MW01600086

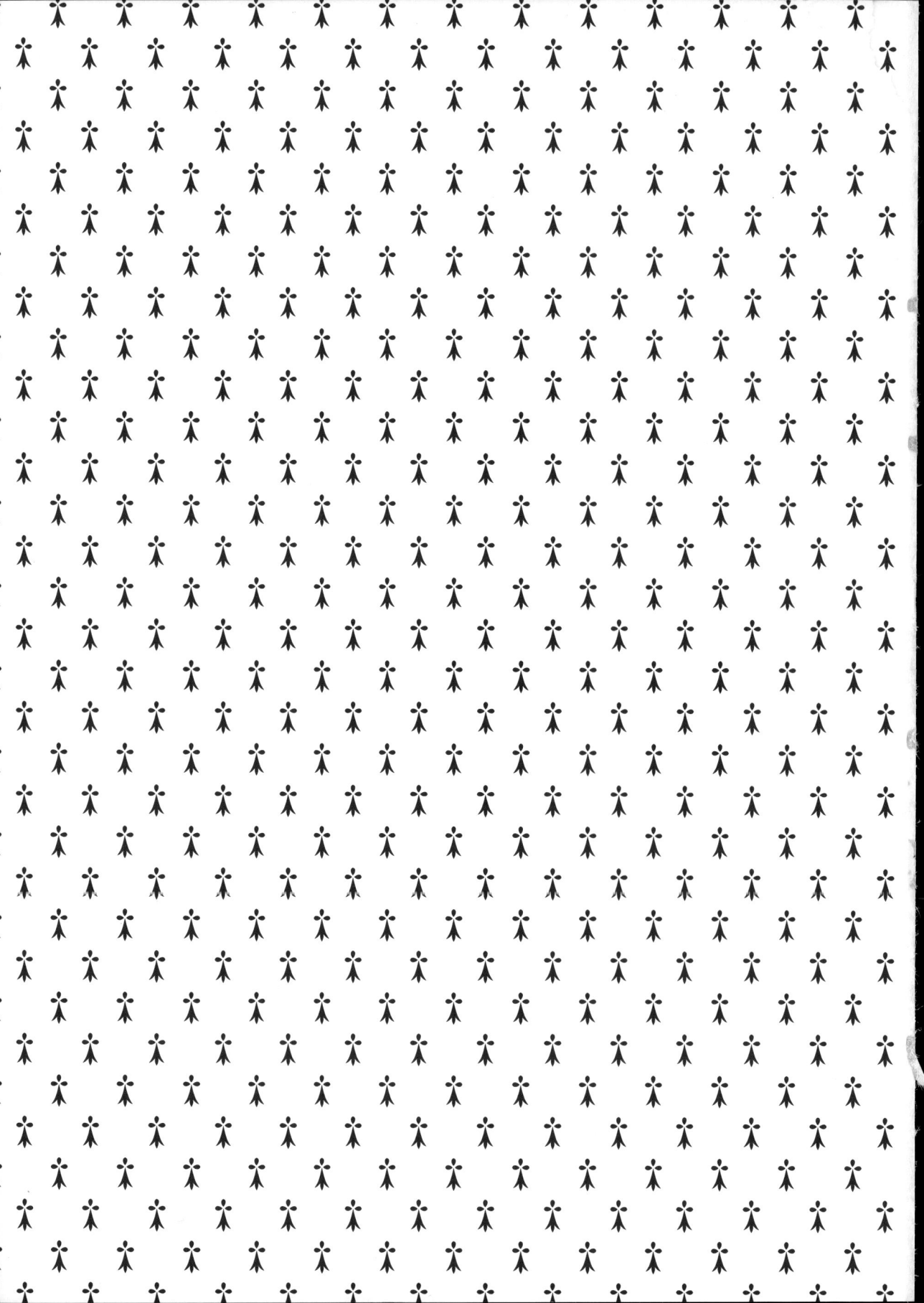

Jan H. Junius

Heraldiek

Amsterdam

Frederik Muller & Cie

MDCCCXCIV.

VOOR ROLF

[1948 † 2010]

FLAG

CREST

SHIELD

JERSEY

BLOOD IN BLOOD OUT

COLLECTION 2005 — 2010

CULTURE FABRICS

BY

IXOPUSADA & FRIENDS

BIS PUBLISHERS

AMSTERDAM © MMX

LEAGUE TABLE

During the European cup of 2004 I was watching the match between Holland and Germany with some friends when suddenly Balázs said he wanted to leave Holland and move to Italy to go and work in Milan. Balázs is not really into football but a discussion came up on what side he should support; either AC Milan or Inter and which shirt we should buy for him to wear. Then it hit me, why not give him a shirt with both sides combined into one?

One year before my father gave me a book that was circulating within my family. It was a manual on Heraldry, the visual language of genealogy. It was the book my grandfather used to produce coats of arms with for people of wealth that wanted to lift their family name up when it did not descend from any nobility. My father helped him out in designing and drawing these composed crests. It felt a bit like a scam.

I went to Malta for a holiday and took it with me to read and study it. This trip turned out to be the ideal combination of research and leisure. As you visit all the historical sightseeing buildings and areas, they are all filled with old publications and artwork of most of the European royal houses on detailed displayed heraldic scrolls as well as visual information on the Templars, the Crusaders and the Roman Catholic Church. Simply a cradle of heraldry. Together with the book I gradually started to understand what this visual language was about and more importantly how one is able to put it into practice.

As a graphic designer most of the time I am dealing with identity. Especially in my free work I try to create and combine identities, making new ones and I experiment with it. Translating cultures into visuals. Playing with simple and strong images like flags, company branding or even iconic imperial eagles as a metaphor for the powers that can be. Perhaps this urge to seek for my own identity derived from my background. I was brought up in the Bijlmer neighbourhood during the Eighties and Nineties, the black suburb of Amsterdam, as one of the few wiggers in the neighbourhood.

It is a pretty old book (*Heraldiek*, Jan H. Junius, Frederik Muller & Cie, 1894 Amsterdam) and it was quite hard to get through as it is written in an older version of Dutch, but for a graphic designer it has turned out to be a real treasure.

Heraldry can be defined as follows:
It is the art of *devising & blazoning* (describing) coats of arms exercised by Heralds and other officers of arms. It was developed in the Middle Ages. Heraldry comes from the Anglo-Norman herald, from the Germanic compound *harjawaldaz*, which means "army commander". The word encompasses all matters relating to the duties and responsibilities of the officers of arms. To most, though, heraldry is the practice of designing, displaying, describing, and recording coats of arms and heraldic badges. Historically, it has often been described as "the shorthand of history" and "the floral border in the garden of history." The origins of heraldry

lie in the need to distinguish participants in combat or tournaments when their faces were hidden by iron and steel helmets. Eventually a formal system of rules developed into ever more complex forms of heraldry.

The Heralds were originally messengers sent by monarchs or noblemen to convey messages or proclamations – in this sense being the predecessors of the modern diplomats. Like other officers of arms, a herald would often wear a surcoat, called a tabard, decorated with the coat of arms of his master. It was possibly due to their role in managing the tournaments of the Late Middle Ages that heralds came to be associated with the regulation of the knights' coats of arms. The primary job of a herald today is to be a creator and thus expert in coats of arms – in that sense being the predecessors of today's graphic designers.

As a designer it means that you have a virtual Legobox with fixed shapes and forms, a fixed number of colours, certain handling rules, little elements as crosses or animals, mottos and ornamental stuff to create a visual identity for someone or something for that matter. It is like making a logo for someone with a certain amount of restrictions.

After the research I started to look for a way and a medium to try to create my own heraldic images and I experimented with different methods to reach a new way of expressing it. The aim was to create a modern version of heraldry by means of procedures I am used to like graffiti or bill-posting posters and lifesize portraits on the street. I really wanted to bring heraldry back as part of streetlife.

Ruud van Nistelrooij scored a tremendous goal making the final score 1 – 1 at full time against Germany. It meant qualification for the quarter finals and, as happy as we all were, it gave me the inspiration to start this new and rather silly hobby of mine. The next day I went to a market to buy a few football shirts. I went for the cheap ones, the fakes you can find at any market or tourist shop, printed with names and numbers. Just to check out what could be possible and to have some shirts that I could mess up without being bothered about. It became pretty clear that the most exciting combinations would be of main rivals. As a Dutchman I felt obliged to make a shirt with Holland and our classic opponent Germany. Another one was England with France. Although it is very slippery fabric to cut and sew with a regular sewing machine I liked the results. But it did not feel real. Not as real as wearing your favourite shirt to expose your roots and pride as I wear Ajax shirts. These first drafts were not something you would really wear and that was the next objective: could I produce shirts that are wearable and reach professional standards? Could they express either an unwearable combination like a political statement or a shirt that someone would really be proud to wear? And could these garments become more than just a football shirt, such as wearable flags or a coat of arms of the total identity of the bearer? Would people see them as accepted multi-cultural garments instead of showing a provocative clash? A lot of people I know have parents of different nationalities. They would not have to choose anymore, they could wear both in one shirt.

The next step was to invest in the real stuff. Luckily I already had a wide collection of shirts I bought in countries I had visited. The latest 'authentic' shirts you buy in a shop for about 70 euros (and they seem to be replicas too as the professional players wear ones with extra layers and tighter cuts. Sometimes they are on the market presented in a box as a limited edition and usually for double the price or more). In the regular football shop in Amsterdam I was allowed to go through their storage and look for older and thus cheaper editions which helped a lot. I asked relatives and friends abroad to send me shirts that were not available in Holland. I also found a tailor around the corner from my studio who was willing to help me out. I was ready to start. I made the first part of the collection consisting of ten or twelve shirts that were divided by the simple and classic divisions in heraldry. Parties per Pale, Parties per Bend and Parties per Bend Sinister. I redid the initial ones I had created using the fake shirts and added shirts like Russia versus Ukraine, Sweden versus Denmark, Turkey versus Greece or Ireland versus England. They were all national shirts and because these shirts do not have any sponsor logos on them (apart from Ireland at the time) the results looked like readymades to me. The next idea was to combine clubs to make city shirts. Even though my friend Balázs decided to go back to his hometown Budapest instead of Milan, the first one I had done was Inter versus AC Milan in a Quarterly. A Quarterly (Party per Cross) is the most common division in heraldry, a follow up of the Party per Pale (vertical line dividing left and right) to avoid cutting through any images charged on a shield before marshalling them. For me it became the best way to express the colours of a city with two rival clubs as it shows one of the identities on either the top left and the bottom right part and vise versa. It makes the combination look like it is bounded

and sort of equal, while the first attempts gave me the feeling of a borderline running through the shirts and by this it showed more of a clash of different cultures.

The project needed a title. As it was all about heraldry, genealogy, blood lines, culture mixing expressed by football apparel and taking all this back to the streets I decided to use the title of a film, a classic in my old neighbourhood, *Blood in Blood Out* (also known as *Bound by Honor*). It is a 1993 crime-drama epic directed by Taylor Hackford. It follows the lives of three Latino relatives, Miklo ("brown from the inside!"), Cruz and Paco in East Los Angeles from 1972 to the mid eighties. I hoped that people who would want to wear my shirts would relate to this title and accept the heraldic content as such. In our appreciation for the film we still shout "Vatos Locos forever!" now and then.

My friend Mathieu Vrijman and his wife Malin Lindmark invited me to join them to do an exhibition during the *European Cultural Capital 2005* in Cork, Ireland. It was the first time I could show my project and they offered me a venue in the Townhall. For a week we were hanging the shirts like banners with fishing threads on the high ceilling of the entrance hall. The installation showed a five versus five country clash with a mixed up referee shirt hanging in the middle. The exhibition was a success; the crowd's reaction was just what I had hoped for. People were talking about unification instead of rivalry and the idea of new flags was interpretated as such. To my suprise, even the 'forbidden' shirt with Ireland versus England was well accepted. Although some people had serious problems with it as they had taken all of the other posters down around town with a picture of this shirt on it.

In 2006 I attended a show at the Leeds Metropolitan University in England where I was a first year teacher in the graphic design department. Thomas Castro from the design agency *Lust* was asked to organize a big exhibition to influence Leeds' art students with work by international artists. The show was called *LSX*. I wanted to show my next few City shirts and I made a special edition for Leeds: Leeds United versus Manchester United, the *Men United Clash*. As I was preparing the installation the staff of Leeds Met enforced me to take that shirt down due to it provoking gestures towards hooliganism on school grounds. I decided to take everything off the walls and give the space to my students for their very first exhibition. While I was taking it down a guy asked me why and after I told him he commented that he did not see it as being a project on rivalry, but, as in Cork, more about brothers in arms. I gave my students the assignment to create their identity on a shirt by using a silkscreening technique, share it with a friend by cutting and sewing, and within a week, we had a new installation up called *Identity 21* and a surprisingly good result of twentyone tailored shirts.

Back in Amsterdam I started to work on a collection that would represent a wide range of heraldic divisions. I used any shirt I could get a hold of and mixed it with a reasonable partner on an international and local level. The shirts were usually mixed to propose a historic event or a European relation, however, more football related content came into play as well. The strict heraldic methods were sometimes bypassed to create a better design or to say something else. Some of them became quite costumy but most of them were made according to the system of heraldry. As I added more and more shirts to the collection, altogether, they began to show a brief view of the history of Europe in stories of war, marriage and current relations between cities and countries over the past few centuries.

In the process I got some other ideas as well, such as, new away shirts for my football team made with heraldic charges. The shapes show the positions of the players within the team formation, the individual expertise. I also started making a few player related shirts on the side. They became heraldic charts of the player's professional career. I have only made a few of some players I admire and if I was able to get hold of a certain shirt or part of it. But it was not the main objective.

In 2008 I was offered to do a 'fashion show', a proper one with catwalk and all, during the *Europe's Night* event in Amsterdam. Each year in May this event promotes the European Union and, according to the *BKB* campaign agency that organized the event, the collection represented this unity. They asked Wilfred Genee, a well known football reporter in Holland, to give heraldic commentaries during the show. It was very nerve racking to do, and we had no time to do a rehearsal, but we pulled it off. The visuals, the music, the lecture, and the models all fit into place. The Dutch Ministery of Foreign Affairs, that supports these events, and BKB were very pleased and asked if they could use the shirts at the next event as background visuals. One minor detail: one shirt was banned again. This time it was a shirt about the Dutch Royal house, which had nothing trivial at all, nore was it provocative in any manner. It was simply a representation of the bloodline consisting of Germany, Holland and Argentina supported with the honour to the Spanish Kingdom. One of the Royals was a visiting guest at the event and therefore certain precautions were taken.

In the same year Nike Sportswear and Show Studio from London asked me to join a group exhibition during *Art Basel* called the *Art of Football*. It was a great opportunity to show the shirts as products of mixing identities. It was during the European Cup in Switzerland and the attendance was enormous. But it was also an eye opener for sports brands to see what could be done with their original apparel. Would they be willing to sacrifice their status and merge with their competitors on a shirt? Can there be a Nike versus Adidas shirt on the market? As the shirts are not about the brands themselves, they are indirectly mixed when you would make, say Holland with Germany. But as professional football is more about which brand will compete against the other, or which brand will deliver the latest football, rather than which teams are playing the cup final, the brands are still reluctant towards mixing their apparel or even collaborating on a production level at all. As long as it is art, a one off, the suggestion is well supported. The brands do like the aesthetics of heraldic divisions. Although you can see similar designs in the history of football shirts, it was seen to be original. After 2008 several designs of the major football brands popped up with similar 'divisioning' of different fabrics within one shirt. It is very complimenting to the project but the fabrics are not 'loaded' with any cultural value. They are just different pieces of fabric put together to create a stylish shirt.

After a few more exhibitions here and there the collection grew bigger and bigger up to a current status of over a hundred and thirty shirts. At these venues people continue to ask me if they can buy them somewhere. I do make personalized shirts on a small scale, but not on a mass production level. And if sports brands will not collaborate to produce these kind of mix-ups why not do it yourself? Last year the idea to make this publication arose in order to promote the project that will hopefully inspire people worldwide to express themselves by mixing cultural fabrics. This era is about multiculturalism anyway, the old nations will graduately fade away. In a few centuries we will all be as mixed as the Brazilians are. We will become one. So why not start now; If you feel like having a unique shirt I hope this book will trigger an urge to make your own wearable flag. All you need are your favourite sides or countries and to divide and connect the best parts in a way so that both or more shirts are recognizable, or simply so that it suits your idea and identity. Just take any compatible garments that are of personal value to you and combine them. Share them with your family, show your descendants in one jersey and wear your family tree on the streets. Take heraldry as an inspiration and then create your own flag, shield, crest, jersey; express yourself, show your colours and wear it with pride.

Floor Wesseling

A BRIEF SUMMARY OF

the Handbook to English Heraldry

WITH ADDITIONAL EDITORIAL

ELEVENTH EDITION

BY

Charles Boutell

LONDON: REEVES & TURNER

1914

RIGHT

LEFT

LEFT

RIGHT

INTRODUCTORY

In the olden time, the Herald's "gentle science," the love of Heraldry, which was prevalent amongst all classes, was based upon an intelligent appreciation of its worthiness. A part of the feudal system of the Middle Ages, and at once derived from the prevailing form of thought and feeling, and imparting to it a brilliant colouring peculiar to itself, Heraldry exercised a powerful influence upon the manners and habits of the people amongst whom it was in use. By our early ancestors, it was the "outward sign of the spirit of chivalry, the index, also, to a lengthened chronicle of doughty deeds." And this Heraldry grew up, spontaneously and naturally, out of the circumstances and requirements of those times. It came into existence, because it was needed for practical use; it was accepted and cherished, because it did much more than fulfil its avowed purpose. At first, simply useful to distinguish particular individuals, especially in war and at the tournament, Heraldry soon became popular; and then, with no less rapidity, it rose to high honour and dignity.

From the circumstance that it first found its special use in direct connection with military equipments, knightly exercises, and the mêlée of actual battle, mediæval Heraldry has also been entitled *Armory*. Men wore the ensigns of Heraldry about their persons, embroidered upon the garments that partially covered their armour, and so they called them *Coats-of-Arms*: they bore these same ensigns on their shields, and they called them *Shields-of-Arms*: and in their Armorial Banners and Pennons they again displayed the very same insignia, floating in the wind high above their heads, from the shafts of their lances.

The Heraldry or Armory of England, an honourable and honoured member of the illustrious family of mediæval European Heraldry, may be defined as a symbolical and pictorial language, in which figures, devices, and colours are employed instead of letters. Each heraldic composition has its own definite and complete significance, conveyed through its direct connection with some particular individual, family, dignity, or office. Every such heraldic composition, also, is a true legal possession, held and maintained by an express right and title: and it is hereditary, like other real property, in accordance with certain laws and precedents of inheritance. But in this respect heraldic insignia are singular and unlike other property, inasmuch as it is a general rule that they cannot be alienated, exchanged, or transferred otherwise than by inheritance or other lawful succession. Exceptions to this rule, when they are observed occasionally to have occurred, show clearly their own exceptional character, and consequently they confirm the true authority of the rule itself. It will be understood, as a necessary quality of its hereditary nature, that the significance of an heraldic composition, while "definite and complete" in itself, admits of augmentation and expansion through its association with successive generations.

THE GRAMMAR OF HERALDRY

The Language of Heraldry — The original language of English Heraldry was the Norman-French, which may also be designated Anglo-Norman, habitually spoken at the Court of England in the early heraldic era. After a while, a mixed language succeeded, compounded of English and the original Norman-French; and this mixed language still continues in use.

Nomenclature — Like its language, *the Nomenclature of English Heraldry* is of a mixed character, in part technical and peculiar to itself, and in part the same that is in common use. Thus, many of the figures and devices of Heraldry have their peculiar heraldic names and titles, while still more bear their ordinary designations. Descriptive terms, whether expressed in English or in French (Anglo-Norman), are generally employed with a special heraldic intention and significance. In the earliest *Roll of Arms* known to be now in existence, which was compiled (as appears from internal evidence) between the years 1240 and 1245, *the Nomenclature* is the same that is found in Rolls and other heraldic documents of a later date. This fact of the existence of a definite *Nomenclature* at that time, proves that before the middle of the thirteenth century the Heraldry of England was subject to a systematic course of treatment, and had become established and recognised as a distinct and independent Science.

Blazon, Blazoning, Blazonry — When a knight entered the lists at a tournament, his presence was announced by sound of trumpet or horn, after which the officers of arms, the official Heralds, declared his armorial insignia—they "blazoned" his Arms. This term, "to blazon," derived from the German word "blasen," signifying "to blow a blast on a horn" (or, as one eminent German Herald prefers, from the old German word "blaze" or "blasse," "a mark" or "sign"), in Heraldry really denotes either to describe any armorial figure, device, or composition in correct heraldic language; or to represent such figure, device, or composition accurately in form, position, arrangement, and colouring. But, as a matter of practical usage, pictorial representation is usually allied to the word "emblazon." The word "blazon" also, as a noun, may be employed with a general and comprehensive signification to denote "Heraldry."

PLACEMENTS & DIVISIONS

The Shield: its Parts, Points, and Divisions — Their Shield, which the knights of the Middle Ages derived from the military usage of antiquity, and which contributed in so important a degree to their own defensive equipment, was considered by those armour-clad warriors to be peculiarly qualified to display their heraldic blazonry. And, in later times, when armour had ceased to be worn, and when shields no longer were actually used, a Shield continued to be regarded as the most appropriate vehicle for the same display. The Shield, then, which with its armorial devices constitutes a Shield of Arms, always is considered to display its blazonry upon its face or external surface. This blazoned surface of his shield the bearer, when holding it before his person, presents (or would present, were he so to hold it) towards those who confront him. The right and the left sides of the person of the bearer of a Shield, consequently, are covered by the right and left (in heraldic language, the dexter and sinister) sides of his shield: and so, from this it follows that the dexter and sinister sides of a Shield of Arms are severally opposite to the left and the right hands of all observers. The Parts and Points of an heraldic Shield, which is also entitled an "Escutcheon," are thus distinguished:—

11 defined points on the field:

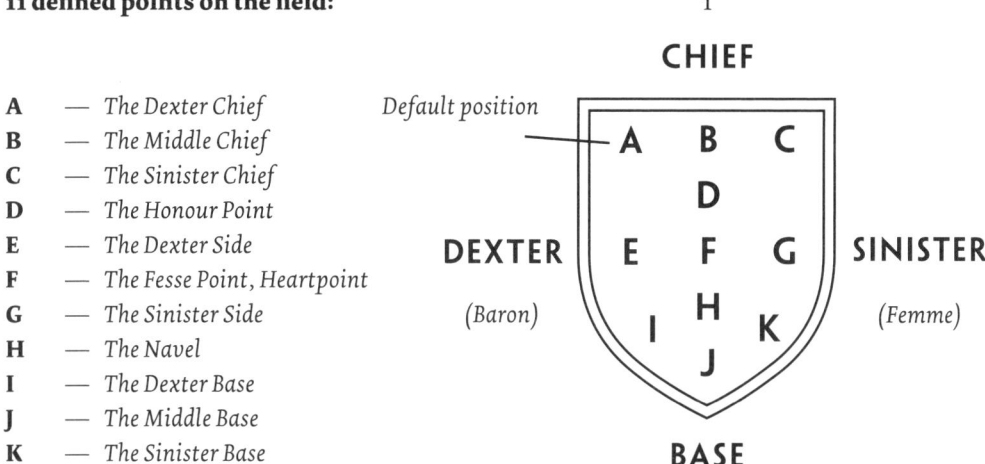

A — *The Dexter Chief*
B — *The Middle Chief*
C — *The Sinister Chief*
D — *The Honour Point*
E — *The Dexter Side*
F — *The Fesse Point, Heartpoint*
G — *The Sinister Side*
H — *The Navel*
I — *The Dexter Base*
J — *The Middle Base*
K — *The Sinister Base*

In blazoning the Divisions of a Shield, the term "Per," signifying "in the direction of," is employed sometimes alone, and sometimes (having the same signification) preceded by the word "parted" or "party." The primary Divisions of a Shield are indicated in the following diagrams, the numbers indicate the order of blazoning:

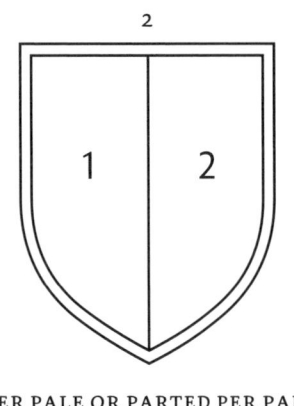

PER PALE OR PARTED PER PALE
OR PARTY PER PALE

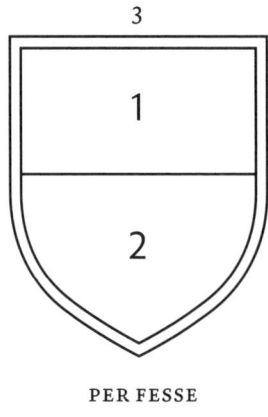

PER FESSE
OR PARTED PER FESSE

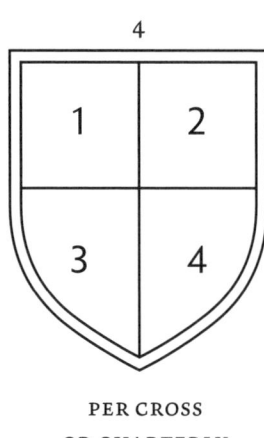

PER CROSS
OR QUARTERLY

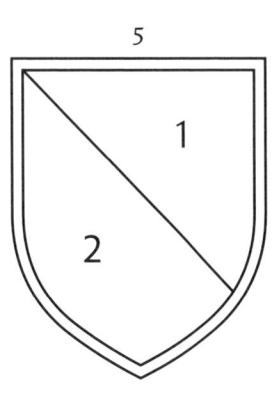

PER BEND

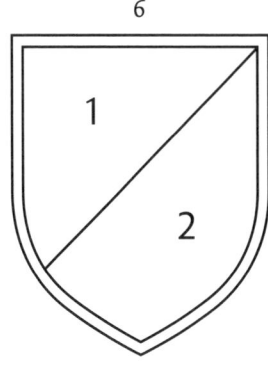

PER BEND SINISTER

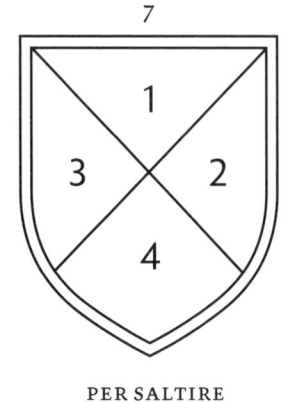

PER SALTIRE

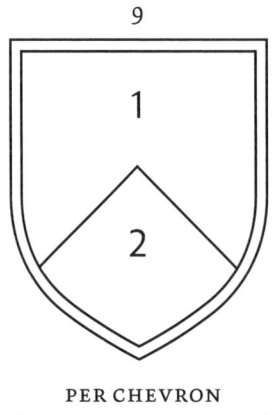

TIERCED IN PALE

PER CHEVRON
(REVERSED IS PER PILE)

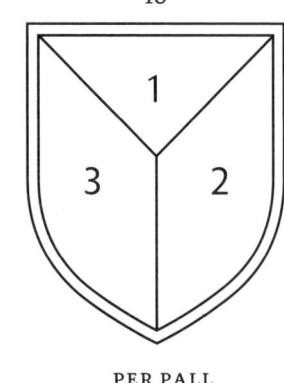

PER PALL

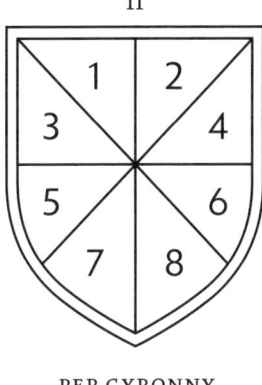

11

PER GYRONNY

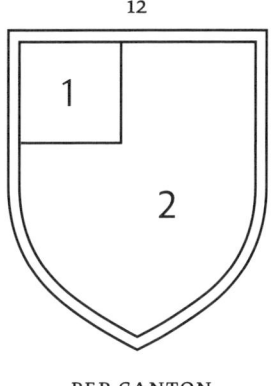

12

PER CANTON

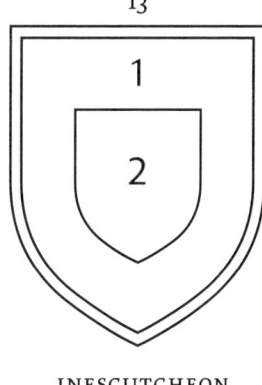

13

INESCUTCHEON

A Shield may be further divided and subdivided, but usually in no more than 16 parties:

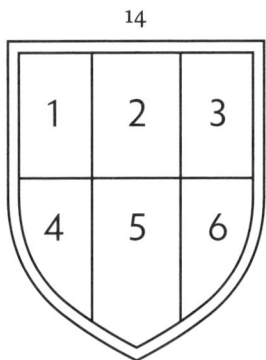

14

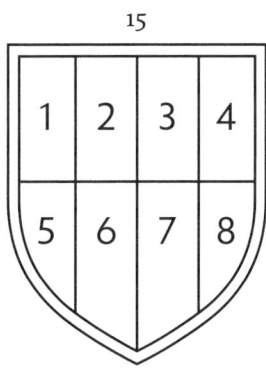

15

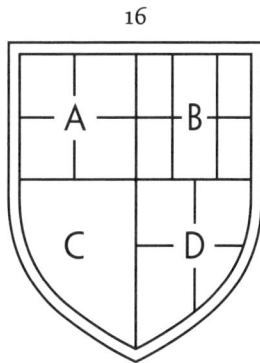

16

It may be divided into any number of *Quarterings* by lines drawn *per Pale* and *per Fesse*, cutting each other, as in No. 14 and No. 15, which Shield is *quarterly of eight*: in like manner the *Quarterings* of any Shield, whatever their number (which need not be an even number), are blazoned as, *quarterly of twelve*, etc. This, to whatever extent the dividing of the Shield may be carried, is *simple Quartering*. Again: a quartered Shield may have one or more of its primary quarters, or every one of them, *quartered*: this, which is the subdivision of a part, the *quartering of quarters*, is *compound Quartering*: for example, in No. 16, the Shield is first divided into the *four primary quarters*, severally marked A, B, C, D; then, so far as the quarters A, B, D are concerned, the "simple quartering" is subjected to the process of "compound quartering," and quarters A, D are *quarters quarterly*, and B is a *quarter quarterly of six*, while C remains unaffected by the secondary process. The terms "quarterly quartering" and "quarterly quartered" are used to signify such secondary quartering as is exemplified in A, B, D of No. 16. The four primary quarters (A, B, C, D of No. 16) are distinguished as *Grand Quarters*: consequently, the quarter B of this example is the *second grand quarter, quarterly of six*. This term "Grand Quarter" may be employed to distinguish any primary quarter when any quarter in the Shield is "quarterly quartered."

Dividing and **Border Lines**, in addition to simple right lines and curves, assume the forms that are represented in the next diagram:

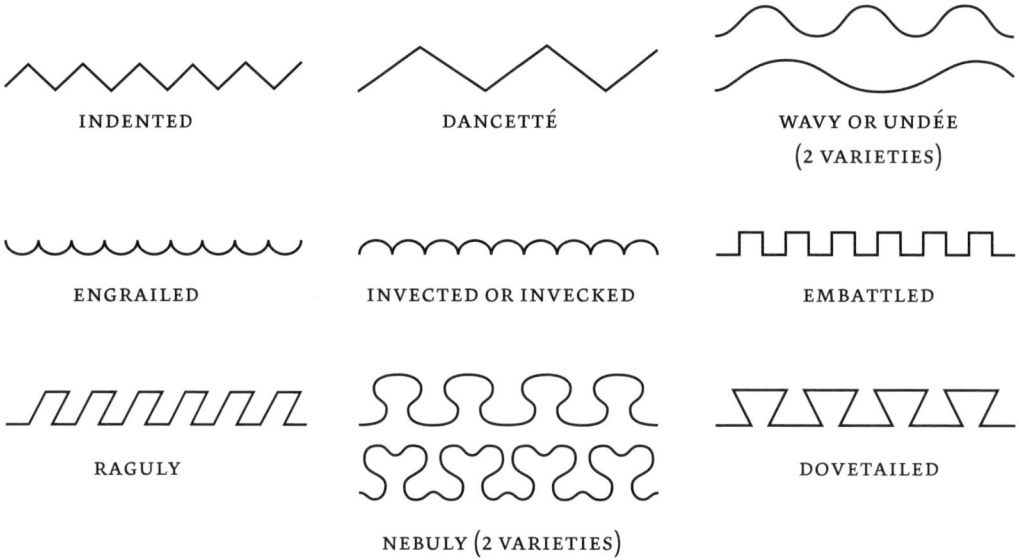

INDENTED	DANCETTÉ	WAVY OR UNDÉE (2 VARIETIES)
ENGRAILED	INVECTED OR INVECKED	EMBATTLED
RAGULY	NEBULY (2 VARIETIES)	DOVETAILED

Two others, less frequently met with, however, are *Rayonné* and *Flory-counter-flory*.

The entire surface of every Shield is termed **the Field**. The same term is also applied to every plain surface. A Shield is said to be "borne" by the personage to whom it belongs: and, in its turn, the Shield "bears" whatever figures and devices may be displayed upon it; whence, all these figures and devices are entitled "Bearings" or "Armorial Bearings." All figures and devices are also styled "Charges"; and they are said to be "charged" upon a Shield, Banner, or Surcoat, or upon one another. In blazoning, the field of the Shield is always first noticed and described: next follow the charges that rest upon the field of the Shield itself; then descriptions are given of the secondary bearings that are charged upon others of greater importance. As a general rule, of several charges which all alike rest immediately upon the field of the Shield, the most important is the first to be blazoned; so that the arrangement of blazoning is determined by the comparative dignity of the bearings, as well as by the degree in which charges are nearer to the field and further from beholders. In some cases, however, a bearing charged upon the field of a Shield and many times repeated on a small scale, is blazoned (for the sake of simplicity and clearness of expression) next to the field of the Shield itself:—thus, if a lion be charged on the field of a Shield, and a considerable number of crosses surround the lion, and, like him, are placed on the field of the Shield also— the field of the Shield is blazoned first, the crosses second, and the lion third; and, if a crescent (or other bearing) be charged upon the lion's shoulder, it is the last in the blazon. In quartered Shields the blazoning commences afresh with each quartering.

TINCTURES

A shield should be recognizable from afar. That is why in heraldry only a select number of colours are used. They are called *Tinctures* or *Enamels*. Colour nuances or pastels are neglected. And the need for contrast makes it unusual to place a colour on another one. In English Heraldry the Tinctures comprise *Two Metals*, *Five Colours*, and the *Furs*. When printed in just black they are symbolised or indicated by dots and lines—a very convenient system, said to have been introduced, about the year 1630, by an Italian named Silvestre de Petrasancta. Some such symbolisation, however, may occasionally be found in anticipation of Petrasancta. The system now in use was not generally adopted till the commencement of the eighteenth century. This system is never officially employed in a matter of record, and is now being discarded by many artists.

The Metals and Colours are named and they are severally indicated, as follows:—

Two Metals:

Gold	*Or*	No. 17	*"Generosity and elevation of the mind."*
Silver	*Argent*	No. 18	*"Peace and sincerity."*

Five Colours:

Red	*Gules*	No. 19	*"Warrior or martyr. Military strength and magnanimity"*
Blue	*Azure*	No. 20	*"Truth and Loyalty."*
Black	*Sable*	No. 21	*"Constancy or grief."*
Green	*Vert*	No. 22	*"Hope, joy and loyalty in love."*
Purple	*Purpure*	No. 23	*"Royal majesty, sovereignty and justice."*

In order to avoid repeating or referring to the word "Or," the word "Gold" is sometimes used. Gold and silver are often visualized as yellow and white. In French Heraldry, Green is *Sinople*.

Two other Colours, or tints of Colour, are sometimes heard of—*Tenne*, a tawny or **orange** colour No. 24 —*"Worthy ambition"* and *Murrey, Maroon* or *Sanguine*, a **dark crimson red** No. 25 —*"Patient in battle and yet victorious"*. These two are sometimes termed *Stains*, but their real usage was in liveries. Animated beings and all objects, that in Heraldry are represented in their natural aspect and colouring, are blazoned *Proper*.

Heraldic charges and compositions, when sketched in outline with pen and ink or with pencil, and with the colours written thereon, are said to be *Tricked* or *In Trick*.

17

OR

18

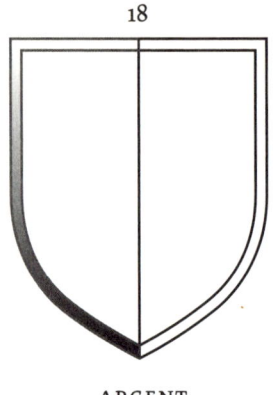

ARGENT

19

GULES

20

AZURE

21

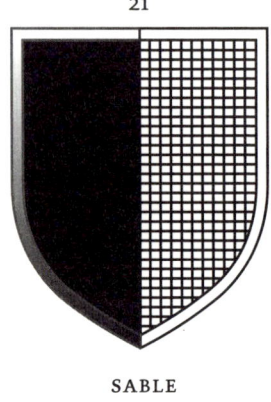

SABLE

22

VERT

23

PURPURE

24

TENNE

25

MURREY

Should the field of any charge be divided into a single row of small squares, alternately, of a metal and a colour, as it is *Componée* or *Compony* (sometimes written *Gobony*): if into two such rows, it is *Counter Compony*: but, if the field of a Shield, or the surface of any charge be divided into three, or more than three, such rows, it is *Chequée* or *Checky*.

The Furs are certain kind of patterns that function as tinctures as well. They are of comparatively rare occurrence, and do not appear in the best ages of Heraldry. Vair and Ermine are common and both furs have their varieties in colour and shape. The mere fact that a shield holds a fur suggests a mark of dignity. In general the fur coat of a weasel is represented for heraldic fur:

Ermine represents the winter coat of the stoat, which is white with a black tail; the heraldic fur is white with a pattern of black spots, representing a number of skins sewn together. (No. 26)
Vair and **Potent** represent a kind of squirrel with a blue-gray back and white belly; sewn together it forms a pattern of alternating blue and white shapes. (No. 27, No. 28)

| 26 | 27 | 28 |
| ERMINE | VAIR | POTENT |

The Law of Tinctures — Every charge is supposed to rest upon the field of a Shield, or on the surface of some charge. It is a strict rule, that a charge of a metal must rest upon a field that is of a colour or fur; or, contrariwise, that a charge of a colour must rest on a field that is of a metal or fur,—that is, that metal be not on metal, nor colour on colour. This rule is modified in the case of varied fields, upon which may be charged a bearing of either a metal or a colour: also, a partial relaxation of the rule is conceded when one bearing is charged upon another, should the conditions of any particular case require such a concession. This rule does not apply to bordures, nor very stringently to augmentations or crests, and it is not so rigidly enforced in Foreign as in British Heraldry. There are, of course, a few exceptions, but they are not numerous, the one usually instanced as an intentional violation being the silver armorial Shield of the *Crusader Kings of Jerusalem* upon which five golden crosses are charged; the motive in this remarkable exception to an established rule being said to be to cause this Shield to be unlike that of any other potentate. What may be termed the accessories of a charge are not included in this law of tinctures: thus, a silver lion having a red tongue may be charged on a blue shield, and the red tongue may rest on the blue field of the Shield.

Should a Tincture or a Number occur a second time in blazoning a single composition, it must be indicated, not by repeating the word already used, but by reference to it. Thus, if the tincture of the field should occur a second time, reference is made to it in the formula—"of the field:" or, perhaps more frequently—"of the first;" or, if the tincture that is named second in order in the blazoning be repeated, it is indicated by the expression—"of the second;" and so on. Again: should there be three fleurs de lys and also three crescents in one and the same composition, having specified the "three fleurs de lys," the number of the crescents would be set forth in the words—"as many crescents:" providing nothing else has in the wording of the blazon intervened in such a way as to cause uncertainty by the use of the term; and so, in like manner, with any other numbers of these or of any other charges.

Emblazoning in Tinctures — On this head I must be content to offer to students only a few brief practical observations. The metal Gold may be rendered with gold prepared in small saucers, or (most advantageously) in minute slabs; this preparation is applied, like a common water-colour, by moistening the gold with water; and it is desirable previously to have washed the paper, card (or vellum) with diluted white of egg. Gold leaf may also be used, but the process is tedious, and requires both skill and experience to ensure complete success. Yellow paint, again, may be used to represent the metal, the best colours being cadmium yellow, or "aureolin" (Winsor and Newton) mixed with Chinese white. For shading, carmine, or crimson lake, mixed with gum. For Silver, aluminium may be used with excellent effect; or Chinese white; or the paper may be left white: for shading, grey (blue and Indian ink mixed) and gum. The Aluminium is prepared, like the gold, in minute slabs: it may be obtained, of great excellence, from Messrs. Winsor & Newton, by whom also a very pure preparation of gold is sold; but both the gold and the aluminium slabs are sold by all good artists' colourmen. These Metals may be diapered, as well as burnished, with an agate-burnisher.

For **Azure**: French blue, freely mixed with Chinese white and a very little gum, the colour to be laid on thick: shade with Prussian blue mixed with a larger proportion of gum.
For **Gules**: Orange vermilion either pure, or mixed with a very little cadmium yellow or Chinese white, and still less gum: (never use a brilliant but most treacherous preparation known as "pure scarlet:") shade with carmine or crimson lake, and gum.
For **Vert**: emerald green, with Chinese white and a little gum: shade with dark green, made from mixing aureolin (or gamboge) with Prussian blue and gum.
For **Purpure**: mix carmine and French blue, with a little gum: shade with a darker tint of the same.
For **Sable**: Very dark grey, made by mixing a little Chinese white and gum with black: shade with black and more gum.

When the Metals are rendered by gold and aluminium, it is desirable that these tinctures should be applied, and that the diapering and burnishing of the Metals should also be completed with the burnisher, before the adjoining colours are laid on. The burnishing may be executed in two or three hours after the Metals have been applied to the paper; and the paper should be placed upon a piece of glass during the processes of burnishing and diapering.

ORDINARIES

The Charges —A charge is any object or figure placed on a heraldic shield or on any other object of an armorial composition. Any object found in nature or technology may appear as a heraldic charge in armory. Charges can be animals, objects, or geometric shapes. The most frequent animated charges are the lion and eagle. Other common animals are stags, wild boars, martlets, fish, human figures, dragons, bats, unicorns, griffins, and more exotic monsters.

The Ordinaries — The simple Charges of early Heraldry, which always have been held in the highest esteem and which are most familiar, are: *the Chief, the Fesse* or *Bar, the Pale, the Cross, the Bend, the Saltire, the Chevron,* and *the Pile.* They may be considered to have been derived from various means that were adopted to strengthen Shields for use in combat, *the Cross* always being in great favour from having a definite symbolism of its own. These Ordinaries may be formed by any of *the Border Lines* (see diagram on page 22). Occasionally they are borne alone; but more generally they are associated with other bearings, or they have various figures and devices charged upon themselves. In some cases, presently to be specified, more than one Ordinary may appear in a single composition. *The Bar, the Pale, the Bend,* and *the Chevron* have Diminutives. *The Cross* has many *Varieties.*

The Subordinaries — This title has been assigned, but without any decisive authority, to another group of devices, second in rank to the Ordinaries. Very few writers agree as to which are ordinaries and which subordinaries; nor does there seem any reason why any distinction between them should exist. Nor, indeed, save that all are exclusively heraldic, why some of them should be regarded as anything more than ordinary charges. These Subordinaries are *the Canton, the Quarter, the Inescutcheon, the Orle, the Bordure, Flanches, the Lozenge, the Fusil, the Billet, the Gyron* and *the Pallium. The Canton,* by the early Heralds commonly styled the "Quarter," sometimes has been grouped with the Ordinaries. And it must here be observed that *the Lozenge, the Fusil, the Billet* and *the Gyron* were not used as single charges by the early Heralds; but by them the fields of Shields were divided *lozengy* and *gyronny,* or they were *semée of Billets,* from which the single charges evidently were afterwards obtained. Each of the above ordinaries is commonly said to take up one-third of the field in theory, though in practice they are usually made somewhat narrower.
Less widespread are *the Flaunches, Pall* and *Pile* (a tapered Pale, pointed at the bottom). *The quarter,* for instance is an upper quadrant of the field, occurs rarely as an ordinary, but its diminished version the canton is frequently found, usually as a mark of distinction (showing that the bearer has no blood relationship to the bearers of the arms without the canton); it theoretically occupies the first third of the chief.
Ordinaries may appear in parallel series, in which case English blazon gives them a different name: more *Pales, Bars,* et cetera are blazoned as *Paly, Barry, Bendlets, Chevronels* and so on.

29

CHIEF

30

FESSE / BAR

31

PALE

32

BEND

33

SALTIRE

34

CHEVRON

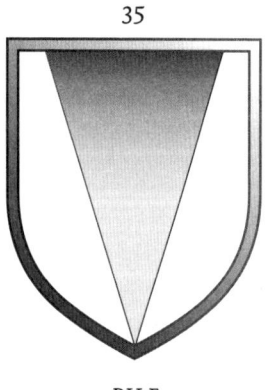

35

PILE

36

CROSS

37

PALLIUM

38

CANTON

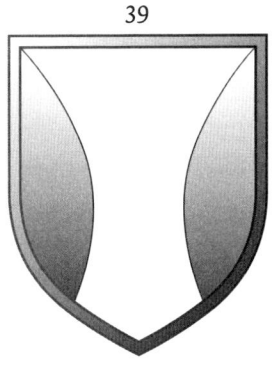

39

FLANCHES

40

LOZENGE

41

FUSIL

42

GYRON

43

BILLET

44

INESCUTCHEON

45

ORLE

46

BORDURE

MARSHALLING

"*Marshalling is a conjoining of diverse Coats in one Shield.*" Upon this concise definition of John Guillim (1551 – 1621) who wrote the book *A Display Of Heraldrie* (1610), in another part of his work, adds the following comment:—"*Marshalling is an orderly disposing of sundry Coat Armours pertaining to distinct Families, and their contingent ornaments, with their parts and appurtenances, in their proper places.*"

Hence it is apparent that this term, "*Marshalling,*" implies:

1. First, the bringing together and the disposition of two or more distinct "*Coats in one Shield*"

2. Secondly, the aggroupment of two or more distinct Coats to form a single heraldic composition, the Shields being still kept distinct from one another: and,

3. Thirdly, the association of certain insignia with a Shield of arms, so as to produce a complete heraldic achievement.

Two or more coats of arms are often combined in one shield; such combination, called marshalling may express inheritance from different families, a sovereign's assertion of various claims, or the occupation of an office by a specific person for the time being. The principal modes of marshalling are:

by Impalement: the shield is divided into right and left halves;

by Quartering: the shield is divided into quadrants;

with an **Inescutcheon**: a smaller shield appears in front of the main shield.

A few very simple diagrams will clearly elucidate the principle of Marshalling the arms of Husband and Wife. Suppose *Baron A* to represent the Husband, and *Femme B* the Wife: then, No. 47 may represent the arms of the Husband, and No. 48 the arms of the Wife. If B be *not* an heiress, the arms of A and B, as husband and wife, are borne impaled, as in No. 49; and their son bears No. 47 only. If B *be an heiress*, the arms of A and B, as husband and wife, are borne as in No. 50 — the arms of the wife on an Escutcheon of Pretence; and, in this case, the son of A and B quarters the arms of both his parents, as No. 51.

Now, suppose this son, whose arms are No. 51, to marry a lady, *not* an heiress, whose arms are No. 52, he would simply impale the arms of his wife, as in No. 53, and his son would bear No. 51 only, as his father bore that quartered shield before his marriage. But if the wife of the bearer of No. 51 were to *be an heiress*, he would charge the arms of his wife in pretence upon his own hereditary paternal Shield, as in No. 54; and his son, by this heiress, as before, would quarter the arms of both his parents, as in No. 55.

It is obvious that Marshalling on this system (of which I here give the general outline) admits of a widely-extended application. Younger sons in all cases place over all the quarterings of their Shield their own distinctive *Mark of Cadency*, until they inherit some different quartering from those to which the head of their house is entitled, and the quartering itself then forms sufficient difference.

47

BARON A

48

FEMME B

49

A & B
IMPALED

50

A & B

51

AB (SON)

52

FEMME C

53

AB & C
IMPALED

54

AB & C

55

ABC (SON)

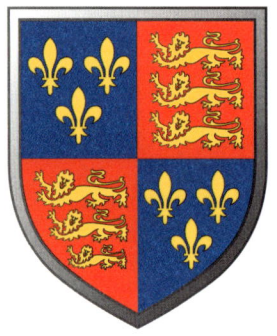

BLOOD IN BLOOD OUT

THE EUROPEAN TOURNAMENT

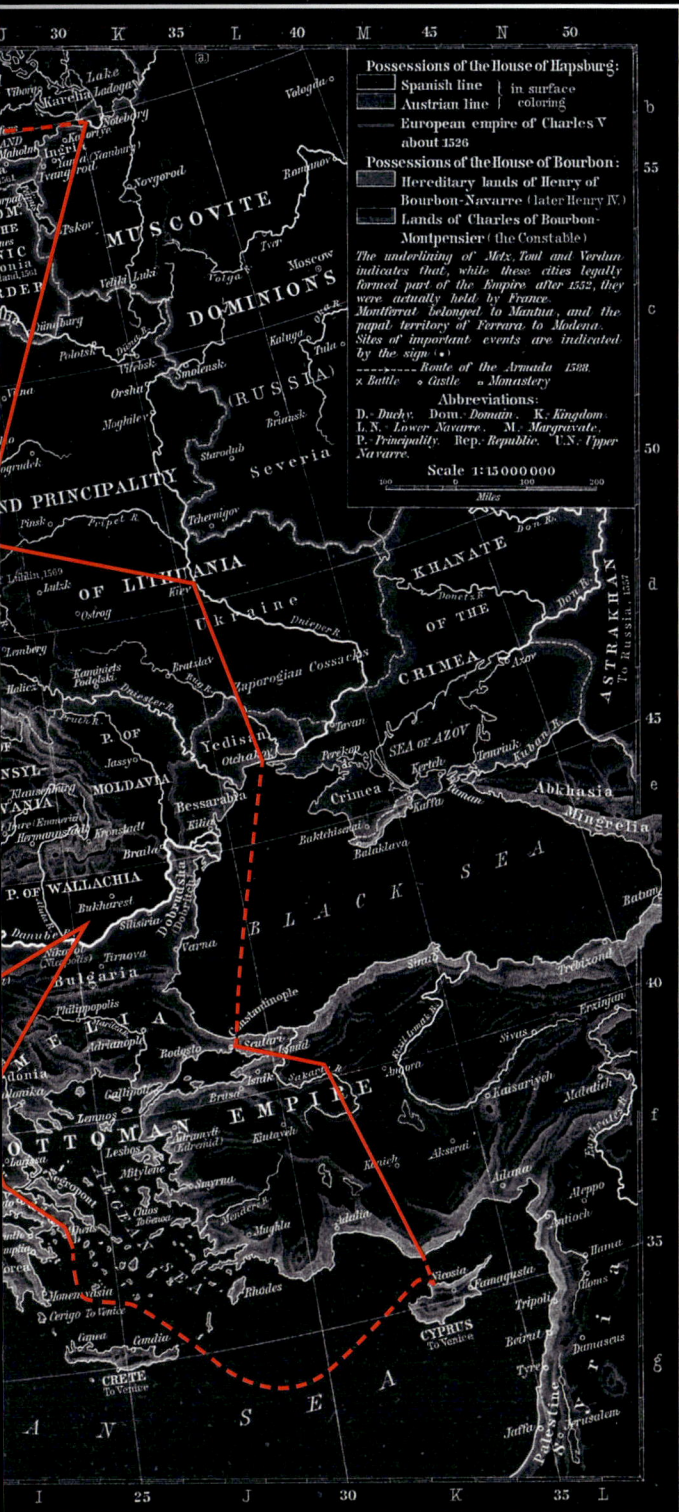

EUROPE

A° 1560

Asia has more people and Africa has more nations. But there is nowhere else on earth where you will find more people and cultures mixed together on such a small stretch of land. Travel through Europe and you will come across so many styles, cuisines, landscapes, subcultures and ancient capitals.

This book gives a brief overview of Europe and its rich history through the lense of modern heralds: the football jersey-bearer. You will learn how the United Kingdoms flag developed over the ages and how this historic process is still depicted in modern day jerseys of clubs like Manchester United and Chelsea.

We come across the battles for freedom and independence of Catalunya and their ties to Cuban revolutionaries. We zoom in on the great derbies of Istanbul, Milan or Hamburg versus Bremen. And we bring back historic processes, like the Union of Kalmar, the Blitzkrieg, the Balkan Wars and the colonisation of the rest of the world.

Follow our trail through Europe and discover the stories that our collection has to offer.

MALTA

Malta has been the scene of fortified European and Arab contact for centuries. Falling into the hands of one great empire after the other, Malta developed a fiercely militarized society. In 1530 Malta came under the rule of the Order of Knights from the Hospital of St. John of Jerusalem. These knights, a military religious order now known as the Knights of Malta, withstood a full-blown siege by the Ottoman Turks in 1565, at the time the greatest naval power in the Mediterranean. The victory granted the Maltese Knights a legendary place in Europe's rich military history. Up to this day the Maltese landscape is dotted with ancient forts poetically named Valetta, Wignacourt and Redin after the Grand Masters who commissioned the work. The Knights of Malta showed their colours with the eight-pointed Maltese cross [left]. Its design is based on crosses used since the First Crusade.

Just as legendary as the Maltese Knights are the Templars: arguably the first multinational cooperation in history. Originally a small and poverty bound group of crusade veterans (hence their emblem of two knights on one horse), the Templars grew into one of the most popular charities in Christendom receiving land, money and sons of noble families. Eventually they counted over 20.000 members. Only 10% of whom were actual knights. The vast majority took care of all possessions. The Templars' existence was tied closely to the Crusades in which they usually formed the advance forces during battles. When the Holy Land was lost, support for the Order rapidly faded. King Philip IV of France, who was deeply in debt to the order, used rumours about the Templars' secret initiation ceremony to persecute them. In 1307, many of the order's members in France were arrested, tortured and burned at the stake. The abrupt disappearance of this once heroic order of knights with their huge properties in the European infrastructure gave rise to speculation and legends. These are the legends that keep the "Templar" name alive into the modern day.

But the Templars were not the only crusaders. What at first glance could be perceived as a unified European and/or Christian wave of religious conquest was actually a deeply divided movement. The reasons to go to the Holy land were as manifold as the number of people going. Most went because they simply had to follow their lord, others went seeking wealth and of course a few went to honour their God and rid the holy sites of the infidels. The distinctive attire of the crusaders, a red St. George's Cross on a lime white field, was taken-up to honour the city of Genoa. It was the city flag of Genoa that was worn because they granted safe passage to the ships bound for the Middle East. Genoa did however get a lot in return; the crusades brought them numerous colonies in the Middle East, Aegea, Sicily and Northern Africa. Moreover, Genoese Crusaders brought home a green glass goblet from the Levant, which Genoese long regarded as the Holy Grail.

Long after the period of the crusades, the Genovese remained a fierce seafaring entity. With Cristopher Columbus as their most famous son, sailing under the Spanish flag straight across the Ocean for India, only to find a whole new world.

taly, a country divided. It was built out of many pieces by the legendary nationalist Giuseppe Garibaldi. As he forced together independent city states, island kingdoms and the vast lands of the Pope, he formed the Kingdom of Italy over the course of the nineteenth century. Nowadays Italy is a powerful nation and a respected founding member of the European Union. But... as Italians share a mighty temper and an ever agitated mood, old and new fights always loom over the Apennine Mountains. It is these mini cold wars that are depicted in this Italian section. The difference in life and economy between the wealthy north and the struggling east; the neighbours at constant war in Milan; all the rival cities with their beautiful emblems going back to their greatness, once.

n the south we come across the demonlike mixture of power, mafia, money and deceit; the Cosa Nostra defying the Berlusconi state. Up north, via mother Rome, we find ourselves in Florence and the Fleur-de-Lys; one of the most notable heraldic charges out there. While the Fleur-de-Lys is often associated with France, it has appeared on countless European coats of arms over the centuries. In heraldry it can simultaneously be political, dynastic, artistic and symbolic. And thus it was used: from Florence to Bosnia and Herzegovina and from the Norroy King of Arms in the United Kingdom to the Swiss municipality of Schlieren. This wide usage only accounts for it being a great insignia. While the Fleur-de-Lys originally symbolized Jesus or the Holy trinity it gradually took on Marian symbolism. In that case the Fleur-de-Lys represents purity and chastity, two things that are widely considered worth fighting for.

n Milan we find the two great football clubs sharing the biggest stadium of Italy, AC Milan and Internazionale. AC Milan was founded as a cricket club in 1899 by British expatriates Alfred Edwards and Herbert Kilpin, who came from the British city of Nottingham. In honor of its origins, the club has retained the English spelling of its city's name, instead of changing it to the Italian Milano, although it was forced to do so during the fascist regime. In 1908, the club experienced a split caused by internal disagreements over the signing of foreign players, which led to the forming of Internazionale.

The most successfull Italian football club Juventus – la Vecchia Signora (the Old Lady) – can be found in another industrial city west of Milan, Turin. It used to be a major European political centre, being Italy's first capital city in 1861 and being home to the House of Savoy, Italy's Royal family. The traditional colour of the national team, azure blue (azzurro, in Italian), is linked to the Royal dynasty: Azzurro Savoia (Savoy Blue). Originally, Juventus played in pink shirts with a black tie, but only because they had been sent the wrong shirts. The father of one of the players made the earliest shirts, but continual washing faded the colour so much that in 1903 the club sought to replace them. Juventus asked one of their team members, Englishman John Savage, if he had any contacts in England who could supply new shirts in a colour that would better withstand the elements. He had a friend who lived in Nottingham, who being a Notts County supporter, shipped out the black and white striped shirts to Turin. Juve have worn the shirts ever since, considering the colours to be aggressive and powerful.

SWISS GUARDS

Well into the twentieth century the Kingdom of Italy more or less shared their flag and heraldy with neighbouring Switzerland. Both had that strong white cross on a red field. Nowadays the bond between the two nations is still upheld by the *Papal Swiss Guard*. The Swiss provided many European Courts with their ceremonial palace guards operating as a medieval kind of bodyguard. The Vatican is safeguarded by them ever since 1506. Swiss Guards have generally had a high reputation for discipline and loyalty to their employers. Apart from household and guard units, some formations have also served as fighting troops; regular Swiss mercenary regiments served as line troops in various armies, notably those of France, Spain and Naples up to the 19th century.

The official dress uniform is blue, red, orange and yellow with a distinct Renaissance appearance. Commandant Jules Repond (1910 – 1921) created the current uniforms in 1914. While a painting of the Swiss Guard bearing Pope Julius II on a litter (by Raphael) is often cited as inspiration for the Swiss Guard uniform, the actual uniforms worn by those soldiers are of the style which appears by today's standards as a large skirt, a common style in uniforms during the Renaissance. A lot of people are under the impression that the uniforms were designed by Michelangelo. But the official *Vatican City Holy See* website recently said: *It is commonly thought that the uniform was designed by Michelangelo but it would seem rather that he had nothing to do with it. However, Raffaello (Raphael) certainly did influence its development, as he indeed influenced fashion in general in Italy in the Renaissance, through his painting.* This seems to suggest that the uniforms were designed by Raphael and not Michelangelo. A very clear expression of the modern Swiss Guard uniform can be seen in a 1577 fresco by Jacob Copp of the Empress Eudoxia conversing with Pope Sixtus III. It is clearly the precursor of today's recognizable three-coloured uniform with boot covers, white gloves, a high or ruff collar, and either a black beret or a black Comb morion (silver for high occasions). Sergeants wear a black top with crimson leggings, while other officers wear an all-crimson uniform.

The marine blue, yellow and crimson red are still reflected in the jerseys and clubcolours of FC Basel, the most succesfull Swiss football team ever. One of the first team captains, Johan Gamper, later founded the great FC Barcelona in 1899. The colours and the emblem of both 'FCB's are very much alike to this day.

The city of Basel and the city of Zürich have a long-standing rivalry. Therefore, FC Basel's most traditional and fiercest rivals are FC Zürich. Supporters from both sides have caused trouble in the past years. The worst incident happened in May 2006. FC Basel had won the league in the 2003/04 and 2004/05 seasons and were set to make it three in a row if they won or drew against Zürich at home on the last day of the 2005/06 season. But if Zürich won, they would get the title. Zürich took the lead after a late goal from Iulian Filipescu and consequently won the match and the league. After the final whistle, players and fans from both teams started fighting on the pitch and in the stands. This incident has fueled hatred and bitterness between fans from FC Zürich and FC Basel.

HABSBURG

The Kingdoms and Lands Represented in the Imperial Council and the Lands of the Crown of Sain Stephen... or if you will Austria-Hungary, the *Dual Monarchy*. It was a vast 19th century Central-Europe an nation, unifying (parts of) modernday Austria, Hungary, Slovakia, the Czech Republic, Ukraine, Ro mania, Croatia, Bosnia and Hercegovina and Serbia. The many peoples ruled by the House of Habsburg never really turned into one nation. The call for more autonomy always loomed overhead. The murder of Franz Ferdinand by Serbian nationalist Gavrilo Princip in Sarajevo in 1914 sparked World War One and brought about the end of the Dual Monarchy four years later. To the right you see a jersey that re sembles the Dual Monarchy and it is charged with the *Patriarchal Cross*, a cross that possesses a smalle crossbar placed above the main one. This variant of the Christian Cross, has its origins in the Byzantine Empire. For a long time, it was thought to have been given to Saint Stephen by the pope as the symbol o the apostolic Kingdom of Hungary. The cross appears in the coat of arms of Hungary and Slovakia.

One of the offsprings of the Dual Monarchy was Czechoslovakia, a state comprised of left overs of its neighbours. Bohemia and Moravia from Austria and Slovakia and Ruthenia from Hungary. From rise in 1918 to fall in 1992, the republic was often under siege; either from outside forces like the Nazis and the Soviets, or from nationalists from different minorities. After the demise of the Soviet Union these seperatists finally had their way and brought a bloodless end to one of the final remnants of the Habsburg Empire.

In the Balkan part of Austria-Hungaria, the proud Serbs were never too happy with their neighbours ruling them. Fortunately for them they have friends in high places; when Serbia is in trouble, it is often Russia that comes to the rescue. Thus also happened in World War One. Besides this Russia also regu arly offers strong moral support. It goes to show that brotherhood is not always defined by geography. A shared language and alphabet mean more when it comes to identity. And a common enemy always helps – the Turks in foregone centuries and the Germans in the bloody twentieth century. Nowadays the recent history of a strong communist rule over multi-ethnic Yugoslavia and Soviet Union strengthen the feelings of a shared background and identity. But how long will this old friendship last, when a future in the European Union draws closer and closer for the Serbs? We might see the Serbs drawing closer to their direct neighbours, once they're back in the European family. Until now though, there has been no ove for the Croats. So close, and yet so far away. They share a border and a language, but their alpha bet is completely different. As is the style and the nature of the people. Serbia and Croatia form a fierce stretch of border between the west and east, between Western-European Christianity and the Ortho dox Church, between the Germans and the Slaves.

Another focal point of animosity is Serbia's southern counterpart. If history teaches us one thing it is that countries that border each other stand a far greater chance to find themselves at war, than coun tries that do not. Imagine the odds when two peoples define the same territory as their cultural heart and. Although a stretch of land far from paradise, Kosovo is the symbol of two national dreams clashing hard. Greater-Albania and Greater-Serbia, both nations from a distant past balance each other in a for gotten part of Europe. They share their cuisine, their music, their culture and even their blood. But it's only when they fight that they truly meet.

CYPRUS

As we follow our trail through Eastern Europe all the way south we find the easternmost EU-country. Or should we call Cyprus a country? Split down the middle between a Turkish and a Greek side. Now that the European Union accepted the Greek side of the island as a full blown memberstate, the Turkish side seems somewhat lost in the far corner of the Meditterranean Sea. Therefore Blood In Blood Out strongly suggests Cypriotic players to use this new jersey from now on and do their part in bringing this lovely land back together.

ISTANBUL

Upwards from Cyprus we pass Asia Minor; with Istanbul as Europe's gateway to the Middle East and the Orient. Much of South-Eastern Europe is defined by centuries of battle between the Turks and the many slavic and germanic peoples. But even with all these historical battles, Istanbul is still a very European city. A city with, like Milan and Madrid, rivalling clubs. Each with their own territory and history; Besiktas on the European side of the Bosphorus, the *Yellow Canaries* of Fenerbahce from the Kadikoy seaside district and the most successful of them all Galatasaray.

UKRAINE

Up from there, across the Black Sea lies Ukraine, a countryname that literally translates to 'Border-land'. This beautiful country to Europe's south-east, overgrown with yellow grainfields under a clear blue sky, is, perhaps tragically, still primarily the land on Russia's border. With almost as much Russians as Ukrainians amongst the population, it's still so hard to let go of one another. NATO, the United States, the European Union may parade their Orange revolutionaries all they want, but they must after all realise that family will not be split.

RUSSIA

The Russian giant meddles in so many affairs. A country of that size on a small continent like Europe almost automatically interferes with all the other nations. With their direct neighbours this is a history of war. With Poland for example the wars turned into outright hatred. But, there are beautiful stories of cultural exchange as well. When Peter the Great set out for his grand tour of Europe he came to the Netherlands to learn all there is to know about building ships. He then also decided to model his flag after the Dutch one, with horizontal stripes, making it clearly visible at sea even in the absence of wind. A century and a half later Russian tsarina Anna Paulowna married the Dutch King William the Second, giving a fair portion of Russian blood to the current Royal House of Orange.

SCANDINAVIA

Before 1397 the Northern countries excelled in turmoil, wars and intrigues. Countries fought councils, aristocrats fought kings, merchants fought cartels and religious leaders fought heretics. The arctic states were on fire.

KALMAR

Finally Queen Margaret, a daughter of King Valdemar IV of Denmark, rose to the occasion and united the three kingdoms of Denmark, Norway and Sweden and the territories of Iceland, Greenland, Faeröer, Orkney, Shetland islands and parts of Finland under one single monarchy. The *Kalmar Union* was born. It was in a way formalized on June 17, 1397 by the *Treaty of Kalmar*, signed in the Swedish castle of Kalmar, on Sweden's south-east coast, in medieval times close to the Danish border. The treaty stipulated an eternal union of the three realms under one king, who was to be chosen among the sons of the deceased king. They were to be governed separately, together with the respective councils, and according to their ancient laws, but foreign policy was to be conducted by the king. It has been doubted that several of the signatories were personally present (for example, the entire Norwegian "delegation"), and it has been argued that the Treaty was only a draft document. It seems to be an ascertained fact that the treaty was never ratified by "constitutional" bodies of the three kingdoms. So, technically the countries had not given up their sovereignty, nor their independence, but in practical terms, they were not autonomous and an era of peace and rest for the population of the new union started. In many ways this bond was the first European Union.

SWEDEN

But such a good thing is not meant to last. Much as the Union united the states, the identities of their people remained incompatible. As the Danish strove for a more centralized government, the Swedish satisfaction with the Union gradually dimished. Early in the 16th century, the Union broke apart and the northern territories fell back into internal warfare.

After the Kalmar Union the Swedes became the dominating power in the north. Ruling amongst others their eastern neighbour with a iron fist. By oppression and force they made it clear that Finnish grounds were rightfully theirs. Over time Swedish became the dominant language of nobility, administration and education, while Finnish was banned from public life and only spoken by the peasantry and clergy. Now independent and rid of foreign dominance the Fins must still be weary of their mighty neighbours.

THE GERMANS

The story of modern European absolutism in violent expansion is perhaps best told by the story of the countries at it's centre; Germany and Poland. For nearly two centuries the history of Poland has predominantly been shaped by it's two great neighbours Germany and Russia. After coming under Prussian regime in 1795 is has only been truly independent in the interbellum. All other phases of either German or Russian turmoil have influenced Poland. When its neighbours grew, Poland shrank.

BLITZKRIEG

This is as much a Polish story, as it is German and for that matter Western-European. As the German war-machine raged over large parts of Europe twice in three decades, countries changed and identities were altered forever. The jersey to the right follows one of the traditional heraldic structures. But it also depicts the schematic approach of the Blitzkrieg (in German: "Lightning War"). Fierce assaults piercing deep into enemy territory with forward armies, meeting only far behind enemy lines and thus surrounding the hinterland in between. As opposed to fighting along one straight front. The Germans referred to a Schwerpunkt (focal point) in the planning of operations; it was a center of gravity towards which was made the point of maximum effort, in an attempt to seek a decisive action. Ground, mechanized and tactical air forces were concentrated at this point of maximum effort whenever possible. By local success at the Schwerpunkt, a small force achieved a breakthrough and gained advantages by fighting in the enemy's rear. It is summarized as "Nicht kleckern, klotzen!" (Don't fiddle, smash!). Spectacular as it was, the Blitzkrieg finally resulted in a break up of the German Heimat with the Berlin Wall as its perfect symbol.

KRIEGSFUSS

Just like any other country the Germans have their regional and local feuds. Munich with its heavy weights FC Bayern München versus the small but much older TSV 1860 München. The derby of the Ruhr area (der Kohlenpott) between Schalke 04 and Dortmund and the great fight of the north (de Nordderby) between Werder Bremen and HSV Hamburg as shown in the jersey with the orange field and the white diamond lines.

In some cases the animosity between the clubs has lead to interesting supporters ties all over Europe. Werder Bremen supporters have a special bond with Udinese fans in Italy. HSV Hamburg and the Glasgow Rangers are tied together by sharing the same colour blue. This in turn sparked strong union between Scottish rivals of the Rangers, Celtic and HSV's adversary in Hamburg, FC St Pauli. The latter, a favourite among Hamburg workers and artists and one of the few clubs to wear the rare colour brown, share their pirates flag with the Celtic supporters.

THE DUTCH

A flag is a powerful thing. It represents identity, independence and pride. Nations will go to war over it and people are willing to die to defend it. The Low Lands had their fair share of struggles and changes of flags. When Prince William of Orange rebelled against the Spanish Duke of Alva, he carried horizontal orange, white and blue stripes. The Dutch people loved it, especially when the Spanish were finally defeated in 1648. The *Prinsenvlag* (the flag of the Prince) was born.

ORANGE

Since then the colour orange became synonymous for rebellion. Over time, the orange Chief was gradually replaced by the red stripe. Most notably because of French control over the Kingdom of the Netherlands. Napoleon Bonaparte's brother Louis made red, white and blue the official flag which is still used today. Be that as it may, two hundred years later orange is still the one colour of national pride.

NASSAU

Another key factor for shaping identity is having an appealing Royal house of Nassau with a fair load of scandals and problems. From the beginning of last century several eccentric figures made their way into the Dutch royal family. A German prince with a taste for fast cars and glamorous women, followed by a modest German diplomat with a public dislike for the necktie. More recently, an Argentinean beauty holding no titles whatsoever joined the Dutch first family to spice up the royal bloodline. All the mixing of blood and people resulted in the eclectic jersey bringing together the Dutch orange, the German white and the Argentinian blue and white in the front, mixing the German Eagle and the Dutch Lion in the back. And still so many Dutch people feel that the Netherlands is not a country for immigration.

MOKUM

Mokum is the Yiddish word for "place" or "safe haven". In Yiddish the names of some cities in the Netherlands and Germany were shortened to Mokum, like Amsterdam, Berlin, Rotterdam and Delft. Today it is still used as a nickname for Amsterdam in a sentimental context, as Amsterdam has always had a big Jewish community. Hardcore Ajax' supporters proudly call themselves *Joden* (Jews), very much appreciated by Israéliens but not that much by Ajax' board. In the Dutch classic, *De Klassieker*: Feyenoord – Ajax, Rotterdam versus Amsterdam, also know as *010 against 020* (district numbers), or even: the hard labourers against the arrogant dandies, the Jewish connotation is used against them.

AMSTERDAM

For a country that is known for its fine trading skills, the Dutch arguably made the worst economic deal in history. At least, that is if you look at it with contemporary eyes. Back then, the trade off with the English was not such a bad thing. In fact, it was very profitable for the Dutch at that time. The small and economically fragile trading post *New Amsterdam* (present day New York) seemed far less profitable than the esteemed riches of the territories in the West Indies. Suriname offered an abundance of coffee, cacao, sugarcane and bauxite.

NEW YORK

The trade off resulted in full colonialisation of Suriname by the Dutch. As the Dutch are known for their major participation in slave-trading, Suriname became populated by many different cultures from all over the world. The Dutch colonisation lasted well into the twentieth century when, in 1975, Suriname was granted independence. Social and economic ties at first remained strong between the two countries. But things took an ugly turn when in the early eighties the capital Paramaribo was the scene of the *December Killings* in which prominent opposition leaders were killed.

PARAMARIBO

Since independence a few hundred thousand people from Suriname, almost half the population, migrated to the Netherlands. Lots of them ended up in Amsterdam; thus bringing a long historical process to full circle: with the 17th century entrepeneurs sailing out from Amsterdam, via the founding of New Amsterdam and the trade off for the colony in South America, onto the 20th century settlement of a large Suriname population in Amsterdam's suburbs, especially the one called:

BIJLMER

As the Surinams migrated to the Netherlands their culture and language enriched this country, especially in the streets of the Bijlmer. *Sranan* or *Sranan Tongo,* is a their fusion language with African, English, Dutch, Spanish and Portugese influences. It is known for its ambiguity. One word can have a lot of different meanings. In this way the slaves had their own secret language that was not understood by the plantation owners. Today Sranan is used as slang by many teenagers all over Holland.

People from Suriname were by no means the only large group migrating to the Low Lands in the past decades. We have seen equally big groups finding their way to the Netherlands as migrant workers and their families from Morocco and Turkey. Much as this is a subject for political controversy in the Hague, it is something that in many ways has culturally enriched the Netherlands.

Up until the Dutch uprising to Spanish, or if you will Habsburg, rule from 1568 until 1648, there were no Netherlands. There were only Northern Low Lands and Southern Low Lands. The first being predominantly protestant and the latter catholic. Nowadays this territory is split into the Netherlands and Belgium. But not strictly along religious lines. Noord-Brabant is a catholic province in the southernmost part of the current-day Netherlands. Now no one would ever want to see the province separate but culturally there are still visible remnants of that old border, like carnaval and an allegedly more Bourgondic lifestyle.

BELGIAN BORDERLINES

In the former southern Low Lands now lies Belgium. As the binding powers, a shared religion gradually dimished, the devisive forces of different languages and cultures gained strength. This last surviving artificially created state in Europe – after the collapse of the Soviet Union, Czechoslovakia and Yugoslavia – is in constant turmoil. The ongoing struggle between Flemish and Wallonians is at an all time high. The language wars have reignited, sparking riots, bringing the Government to collapse and prompting many people to say that the country is finished. Game over Belgium?

HOUSE OF BRITAIN

Being the son of the Duke of Normandy or better known as Robert the Magnificent, you might say that a great future lays ahead. But as an illegitimate child he started out as William the Bastard. It was not until his militairy success that he became William the Conqueror. As a grandnephew of the English Queen, William pressed his claim to the crown, by invading England in 1066. He lead an army of Frenchmen, Normans, former Danish and Flemish men to victory over the English making himself King William I of England and bringing together the Norman-French lands with the British isles. He largely removed the native ruling class, replacing it with a foreign, French-speaking monarchy, aristocracy, and clerical hierarchy. This brought about a transformation of the English language and the culture of England, Wales, Scotland and Ireland.

A few centuries later England was the scene of the *Wars of the Roses*; despite the great name it had no warmth and beauty to it at all. England has a history of civil wars and the Wars of the Roses were fiercy. The houses of York and Lancaster fought each other hard for the throne of England. Both wore a rose as their symbol – a white rose for the House of York and a red one for the Lancasters. After the civil wars the combined red and white rose, remained a symbol for England.

The Gaelic culture of Ireland was, in turn, surpressed by the British and still is. For the Irish Northern Ireland is still a 'province' called Ulster. According to one myth, the kingdom of Ulster had at one time no rightful heir. Because of this it was agreed that a boat race should take place and that *"who soever's hand is the first to touch the shore of Ulster, so shall he be made the king"*. One potential king so loved and desired Ulster that, upon seeing that he was losing the race, he cut off his hand and threw it to the shore – thus winning the kingship. The hand is red to represent that it would have been covered in blood. *The Red Hand* can be regarded as one of the very few cross-community symbols used in Northern Ireland due to its roots as a Gaelic Irish symbol.

The religious animosity between protestants and catholics is still alive throughout the British Isles. For example the city of Glasgow has its very own clash of churches on the football pitch. The blue Glasgow Rangers on the protestant side and the green Celtic catholics. But they do share their main sponsor: Carling Beer. In what is called *The Old Firm*, the heads of both clubs have made a commercial pact with Britains biggest brewery, that their supporters, sworn enemies as they are, will still drink the same beer.

While English power grew and grew it became the United Kingdom of Great Britain and Northern Ireland and its colours are shown by its strong well known flag: the Union Jack. The First Union Jack was produced in obedience to a *Royal Proclamation of King James I* in 1606, to provide a single National Flag for both England and Scotland as a single kingdom. It put an end to certain rivalry between North and South Britain. This "Union" Flag combined the blazonry of the two rival ensigns by blending the cross and the saltire of St. George and St. Andrew. In 1801 the Second Union Jack was created as the "Union" with Ireland was set. The ensign of Northern Ireland was integrated, the St. Patrick, making it the Union Jack of today. The name "Jack" derives from the author of the First Union Flag, King James, who, in the Heralds' French language, would be styled "Jacques": and so the Flag would be called "Jacques' Union,"

LIVERPOOL

Liverpool used to be the major port city of the United Kingdom if not Europe. Trading slaves, materials and other goods with Ireland, the European mainland, the Carribean and the West-Indies, the city grew and grew in importance and size. At the turn of the 18th century over 40% of all world trade passed through Liverpool's docks. Liverpool was even described as the Second city of the Empire by Benjamin Disraeli, the Prime Minister at the time. For periods during the 19th century the wealth of Liverpool exceeded that of London itself. The Liverpudlians did well for themselves. Inhabitants of Liverpool are also known as Scousers, in reference to the local dish known as Scouse, a form of stew.

Then the railways came. Liverpool and Manchester were connected to spread the harbour goods to the towns and mills inland. And after the railways the *Manchester Ship Canal* was built, ships could bypass Liverpool and transport goods directly into Manchester. This caused job losses at the Port and great resentment from the local people of Liverpool while Manchester was taking the supremacy of the North-West. Both the crests of Manchester City and United display a ship representing the Manchester Ship Canal.

This happened at a time when the first official football clubs and leagues were starting and the rivalry between the two cities exploded on the pitch. The greatest English classic was born called the:

RED WAR DAY

Once upon a time in Croxteth, a new king was born. The King of Crocky. He ruled the grounds of Everton but found treasure at Old Trafford. It was there in Stretford where he finally took care of the old rival Reds. As he used to wear Everton blue his hatred towards the Reds is understood. Now being a Red Devil from Greater Manchester his army was strong enough to beat the rival Reds and he finally could as United rules.

MANCHESTER

The name Manchester originates from the Ancient Roman name Mamucium, the name of the Roman fort and settlement, generally thought to be a Latinisation of an original Celtic name, possibly meaning "breast-like hill" from *mamm*, "breast", plus Old English *ceaster* which means "town", which is derived from Latin *castra,* "camp". An alternative theory suggests that the origin is British Celtic *mamma* which means "mother", where the "mother" was a river-goddess of the River Medlock which flows below the fort. *Mam* means "female breast" in Irish Gaelic and "mother" in Welsh.

CITY

Manchester City's first known competitive fixture was played in November 1880, when the side was known as St. Mark's (West Gorton), they then became Ardwick Association Football Club in 1887 before changing their name to Manchester City Football Club in 1894. The City fans' song of choice is a rendition of "*Blue Moon*", which despite its melancholic theme is belted out with gusto as though it were a heroic anthem. City supporters tend to believe that unpredictability is an inherent trait of their team, and label unexpected results "*typical City*". In the late 1980s, City fans started a craze of bringing inflatable objects to matches, primarily oversized bananas. A common stereotype is that City fans come from Manchester proper, while United fans come from elsewhere. Before the Second World War, when travel to away games was rare, many Mancunian football fans regularly watched both teams even if considering themselves "supporters" of only one. This practice continued into the early 1960s but as travel became easier, and the cost of entry to matches rose, watching both teams became unusual and the rivalry intensified.

UNITED

Manchester United is one of the most successful clubs in the history of English football and with nearly five percent of world's population supporting them (330 million people) they could be called the biggest club in the world. Manchester United started out as the *Newton Heath Lancashire and Yorkshire Railway Football Club* in 1878. The first team was formed by a railway engineer from – how ironic – Liverpool named Frederick Attock. They played in green and gold kits. In January 1902, with debts of £2,670 (equivalent to about £210,000 in 2010) the club was declared bankrupt. After seeking new investment, four local businessmen, found by captain Harry Stafford, invested £500 each in return for a direct interest in running the club, and it was decided that the club should change its name; on 26 April 1902, Manchester United officially came into existence. Now that Manchester United faces financial turmoil again at the hands of their American big-money owner, Malcolm Glazer, the old homey green and gold finds its way back to the stands.

WE ARE JUST ONE OF THOSE TEAMS
THAT YOU SEE NOW AND THEN
WE OFTEN SCORE SIX
BUT WE SELDOM SCORE TEN
WE BEAT 'EM AT HOME
WE BEAT 'EM AWAY
WE KILL ANY BASTARDS
THAT GET IN OUR WAY
WE ARE THE PRIDE OF ALL EUROPE
THE COCK OF THE NORTH
WE HATE THE SCOUSERS
THE COCKNEYS OF COURSE
WE ARE UNITED
WITHOUT ANY DOUBT
WE ARE THE MANCHESTER BOYS

UNITED SOUL
IS NEVER SOLD
SO PROUDLY WEAR
THAT GREEN AND GOLD
WE'LL NEVER WEAR
OUR FAMOUS RED
TILL GLAZER IS GONE
OR EVEN DEAD
SO RAISE THAT ANCIENT
STANDARD HIGH
BY GREEN AND GOLD
WE'LL LIVE OR DIE
THAT DAY
WILL COME FOR SURE
WHEN WE CAN WEAR
OUR RED ONCE MORE

LONDON CALLING

Moving down to the south of the country, we come to London town, the capital city of England. Roman London (known then as *Londinium*) inhabited just a very small area of what is now known as the City of London. Since then the city has been home to Anglo-Saxons, Vikings, Normans, Tudors and Stuarts. Despite its rocky history made up of invasions, great plagues in which almost half of the population died, fires destroying most of the city, and famine, London has fought through and come to be amongst the most influential commercial, politcal and cultural hubs across the globe today. The romans built the famous London Wall as defence around the city, although, at present there are scarse remains demonstrating that it ever existed. The sixth century saw the arrival of the Anglo-Saxons who contructed another settlement just a mile away from the primordial Londinium. The Vikings invaded during the ninth century and the Normans. During medieval times, London grew fairly rapidly. By the nineteenth century, London was the capital of the prodigious British Empire; thus was transforming into a hotspot for immigrants from both Europe and the Colonies. The twentieth century too saw continued immigration from Commonwealth countries converting London into the multicultural haven it is today. The coat of arms is white and red with a sword representing the death of the city's Patron Saint (Saint Paul). Below, London's latin motto, states; *"Domine dirige nos"* meaning "Lord, guide us". London's gradual expansion over the centuries now means it boasts 32 boroughs. This extension is known as Greater London and conveniently permits tantalizing derbies in football. London has thirteen League football clubs, including five in the Premier League: Arsenal, Chelsea, Fulham, Tottenham Hotspur and West Ham United.

The North London derby is the name of the football local derby between the two major teams in North London – Arsenal and Tottenham Hotspur. It specifically refers to individual matches between the teams, but can also be used to describe the general ongoing rivalry between the clubs. Tottenham Hotspur Football and Athletic Club was founded in 1882 by a group of boys from Hotspur Cricket Club and school. Its original name was Hotspur FC, but was modified a couple of years later. The club's colour was navy blue, nonetheless, other colours have been introduced since, such as, red and white. In 1895 Tottenham Hotspur turned professional and has been a remarkably strong London based team. 1963 saw them win The European Cup – Winners Cup making them the first British club to win a major European competition. Arsenal, on the other hand, originated slightly later at the end of 1886. Amusingly by a group of Scotsmen! Despite starting out after Tottenham, Arsenal turned professional four years previous. The original kit consisted of a dark red long sleeved shirt with a collar and three buttons down the front, (seemingly not practical) and white shorts. Arsenal has stayed loyal to the colour red to this day. *Curiously, in 1887, Arsenal and Tottenham met for the first time. Unfortunely, due to darkness, the match was abandoned fifteen minutes prior to time. Spurs had been leading 2-1, perhaps this was the moment a friendly rivalry was initially provoked.* A proper rivalry between the two teams did not begin until 1913, when Arsenal moved from the Manor Ground, Plumstead to Arsenal Stadium, Highbury, just four miles from Tottenham's White Hart Lane; by doing so, they became Tottenham's nearest neighbours and thus began a natural local rivalry.

We cross the Channel into fashionable Paris and further south, with Paris Saint Germain versus Olympique Marseille and the Olympique Gymnaste Club de Nice versus AS Monaco; all cities right fully associated with the good life. So, resembling 'The Good Life' is easy when you look great, and Paris, Europe's fashion capital, is most definately a city where you can find people 'living well', or at least looking that way. Fashion and football are regularly referred to at the same time, not solely due to most footballers having high profile fashion icons for girlfriends or wives, but fashion has gradually developed alongside sport. It has come to be more practical and the use of sportswear as leisurewear is not out of the ordinary nowadays. By simply taking into consideration the countless styles and colours of trainers available on the market, the depths at which fashion designers go to is clear and we can see that practicality is not always the key when designing sports attire. So where do the boundries of fashion and sport now lie? It could be said that both have been able to learn from each other: fashion now delves into protection and practicality more readily and sportswear has experimented with decorative ways in creating garments. The current challenge to produce designs that are, in some cases, not only practical, yet, aesthetically pleasing at the same time has been brought closer to the surface by fashion and sport.

Travelling from one glamorous location to another, we find ourselves in Monaco, often referred to as the European equivalent of Las Vegas. It is the second smallest country (after the Vatican City) in the world. Subsequent to the Genoese settlement there in 1215, the Grimaldi family took control in the late thirteenth century and a kingdom was established in 1338. Towards the end of the nineteenth century, Monaco enjoyed promising economic development and, since then, has continued to offer its magnificent scenery, trendy casinos and mild climate making it a world famous tourist destination for upper class travellers. In 1924, just as Monaco's economy had been prompted, its football club Association Sportive de Monaco (shortened to AS Monaco) was founded. It is the only football club outside of France to have participated in the french football system and it has been one of the most successful. The club is known as *Les Rouge et Blanc*; (Red and whites) hence the colours.

Moving just very slightly down the coastline we arrive to the fifth largest city in France, Nice, which is believed to be one of the oldest human settlements in the world. The city is the second most popular tourist destination in France and, as with Monaco, attracts an abundance of wealthy tourists to its attractive coastline and luxurious ambiance. In the early twentieth century, The Gymnastic Club Nice was set up aiming to encourage athletic activity in general with its original colours being black and blue. Fifteen or so years later, the club absorbed Gallia Athletic Football Club, took on red and black and ditched the colour blue. The club's crest is representative of Nice and much like its coat of arms including a black eagle with a red crown. In 1924, the club's name was changed to Olympique Gymnaste Club Nice, and that was the start of another great journey in the history of French football clubs. Local derbies are popular in France, and at just 18 kilometres apart, AS Monaco and OGC Nice are perfect (if there ever existed) rivals. Matches between the two clubs are considered important events and spark a magical and exciting atmosphere.

IBERIA

The Iberian Peninsula lying splendidly in the far South-Western corner of Europe, with its wide array of ancient kingdoms, powerful cities and strong traditions. The outsider sees Spanish unity; both a strong player in international politics and a world power in sports. The players of the European football champions however come from completely different backgrounds, socially, geographically, politically. More than other European countries, Spain has a history of pluriformity.

HOUSE OF SPAIN

Internal borders between Spanish kingdoms like Navarra and Aragon are still more than signpostings by the road. They refer to territories that have their own specific characteristics; in terms of food, celebrations, etcetera. The inhabitants of these former entities still take pride in this background, that they feel is distinctly theirs.

And then there are the ethnic differences. After centuries of Spanish unity it's highly questionable whether these distinctions really can be made, but many people clearly still feel them. This goes for example for the Basques in their districts on the French-Spanish border and for the Catalunyans in the north-east. These ethnic tensions are further strengthened by the rivalries of the Spanish Civil War where communist Catalunyans fought Franco's fascist centralists from Madrid. Of course this was all long ago, but during the matches between Real Madrid and FC Barcelona history definitely comes alive. Amongst other things this is shown by the use of the *Senyara*, one of the oldest known flags worldwide, According to a legend the Senyera was already used in the eleventh century. The red stripes symbolize the traces of the blooded hands of Raymond Berengarius II of Barcelona on the golden tunic of his oponent and murderer. Since the beginning of the twentieth century the Senyera is used by Catalonian Nationalists. Nowadays the *Estelada Blava*, a variant of the Senyera superimposed by a blue triangle and white five-pointed star, is the most notable flag symbolising the national freedom and independance for Catalunya. The inspiration for which, interestingly came from early twentieth century Cuba that was then still de-facto under power of the Americans. Cuba's fight for its independence was followed with attention by the Catalanists of the nineteenth century. The provisional *Constitution of the Catalan Republic* was written and approved in 1928 in Cuba by the *Constituent Assembly of Catalan separatism*.

PORTUGAL

The only people in the Iberian Peninsula managing to withstand Spanish centralist power are the Portuguese. And naturally so, as Portugal dates back to ancient times and was a formidable player in the late middle ages and Renaissance era, building a vast colonial empire lasting well into the twentieth century.

OVERSEAS

This world is big! To big for us to zoom in on all the beautifull background stories of great derbies and historical connections finding their way onto the football pitch. But we have taken the liberty to present to you some of the associations we have, when looking beyond the ocean.

Some countries just have trouble letting go of their colonies. And in the case of Portugal, who can blame them for holding on to most of them way into the seventies? Cabo Verde, Mocambique, Angola, territories that hold this vague promise of paradise and strangely appealing danger. Both in the former colonies as in Lisboa the former masters and their servants make for a beautiful mix.

The rivalry between Brazil and Argentina dates back to the twenties of the 19th century when they fought over the "Eastern Shore" – what we now call Uruguay. Nowadays the battle moved to the football pitch. Being foodball worldpowers, they've produced an enormous amount of players that changed the face of the game. Sports is an escape for the youngsters living in slums and dealing with poverty every day. The dream of once boasting the colours of their country, light-blue and white and canary-yellow in the football arena, is often the one thing keeping them alive.

Remember the Falkland Islands? This small group of islands in the South Atlantic Ocean lies firmly in the hands of the United Kingdom. Much to the chagrin of its large neighbour Argentina that claimes sovereignty ever since 1833. This stance even led to an invasion in 1982, but that turned into a great disapointment for the warmongerers in Buenos Aires. A historic military failure made up for only in 1986 by Maradonna's 'hand-of-god' goal against the English imperialists in the Mexico World Cup.

The immaculate white of the United States' jerseys contrasts starkly with the bright green of its southern neighbour and the Kremlin dark red of its Russian antipode. The Americans hold the globe, but can they own the pitch as well?

China and Japan; the two giants of Asia, home to almost a quarter of all human beings. Of all the jerseys in this book, probably most people feel somehow represented by this one. Although how deep is the love for one another? From our distant European viewpoint China and Japan seem like two of a kind, tucked away in the far corner of the world. But the differences between the two are abundant. An endless history of small fights and all out wars culminating in two opposing economic systems. For decades Japan seemed the clear winner of the two, but as the economic crisis still rages on, it now seems to be China that takes home the prize.

The last jersey is not a football jersey. This is the history and future of cricket in one shirt. The three leading nations of the sport; once united in one empire, now forever free to live and be as they please. Free to play that same old sport against that same old enemy. If you bring together the three flags of India, Pakistan and England, only India survives...

TEAM

PLAY UP AND CLAIM THE GAME

I PLAY FOOTBALL AT ZEEBURGIA,
THE SECOND SENIOR TEAM ON SATURDAYS.
WE ARE A GROUP OF FRIENDS WITHOUT A MANAGER.
BUT WE ARE A TEAM. WE ARE A GOOD SIDE. USUALLY
WE ARE LUCKY. BUT IF WE LOSE WE LOSE BADLY. MOST
OF THE TIME IT IS DUE TO OURSELVES. OR THE REFEREE
OF COURSE. LAST YEAR WE WON THE LEAGUE. THE
FIFTH CLASS, NUMBER 504, DIVISION WEST II THAT IS.
WE ARE WELL PROUD ALTHOUGH THIS YEAR THINGS
ARE LOOKING WORSE FOR THE REIGNING CHAMPION.
SOMEWHERE BELOW ON THE TABLE. FOR SOME NEW
SPIRIT NEXT SEASON WE HAVE A NEW KIT. THE SHIRTS
SHOW OUR POSITIONS INSTEAD OF NAMES. ALL FOR
ONE AND ON FOR ALL WE PLAY OUR FORMATION AND
WIN THE BALL. KEEN ON INDIVIDUAL EXPERTISE.
WE PLAY UP AND CLAIM THE GAME.

KEEPER

RIGHTBACK

LEFTBACK

SWEEPER

CENTERBACK

DEFENSIVE MIDFIELDER

ATTACKING MIDFIELDER

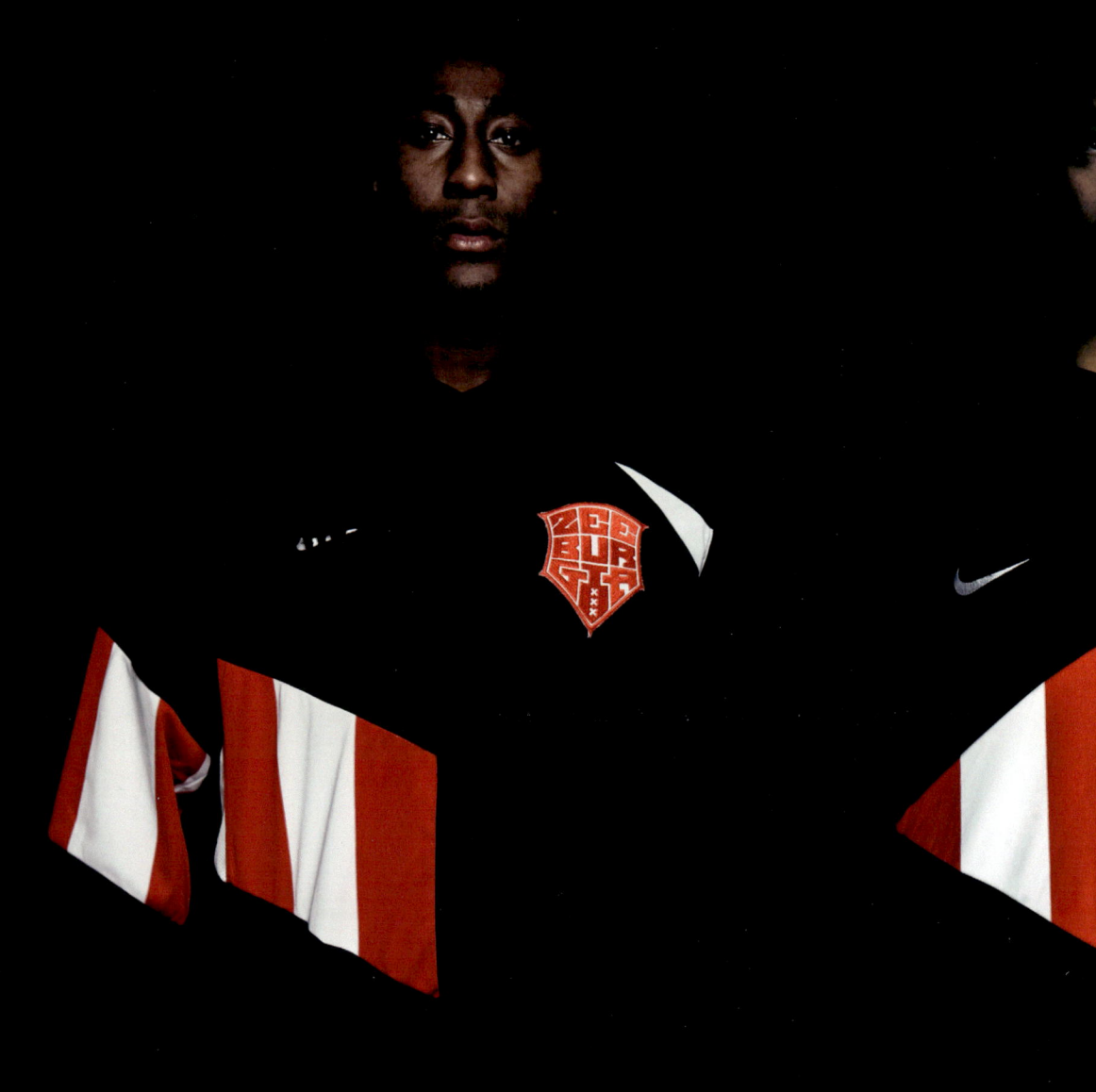

RIGHT MIDFIELDER ━━━ CENTER

4 – 3 – 3

4 - 4 - 2

REFEREE

1 — PAGE 38	2 — PAGE 40	3 — PAGE 41	4 — PAGE 43
Malta	*Colombo*	*San Giorgio*	**Sicilia**
Spain (H), England (A), France (3rd) and Turkey (H) quarterly charged with cross Maltese argent (irreg. gules to gules)	Italy (H) charged with English badge in chief, Atlético Madrid (H) parted per pile	Internazionale (H) and AC Milan (H) quarterly, charged with fesse Sampdoria (H)	Italy (H) and US Città di Palermo (H) parted per bend

5 — PAGE 46	6 — PAGE 47	7 — PAGE 50	8 — PAGE 51
Cosa Nostra	*Giovani Falcone*	*Roma*	*Fleur-de-Lis*
US Città di Palermo (H) and AC Milan (H) parted per bend	US Città di Palermo (A) charged with pale argent (sinister cut off)	AS Roma (H) charged with pale SS Lazio (H)	ACF Fiorentina (H) charged with lozenge France (H), charged with Fleur-de-lis in gold

9 — PAGE 52	10 — PAGE 53	11 — PAGE 54	12 — PAGE 55
Forza Italia	*Milano*	*Derby d'Italia*	*Derby d'Italia deluxe*
AC Milan (H) and Italy (H) parted per bend	Internazionale (H) and AC Milan (H) quarterly	Internazionale (H) charged with bordured counter chevron Juventus FC (H)	Juventus FC (A) and Internazionale (H) per pale, sable neutral parted per pile

13 — PAGE 57	14 — PAGE 58	15 — PAGE 58-59	16 — PAGE 59
Casa Savoia	*Zürich*	*Blaugrana*	*Basel*
Italy (H, *Confederation Cup*) charged with lozenge Switzerland (H), charged with cross argent	FC Zürich (H) and FC Basel (H) parted per fesse	FC Basel (H) and FC Barcelona (A) quarterly	FC Basel (H) and FC Zürich (H) parted per fesse

17 — PAGE 61	18 — PAGE 62	19 — PAGE 63	20 — PAGE 64
Habsburg	*Sudetia*	*Czechoslovakia*	*Serbs of Croatia*
Hungary (H) and Austria (A) parted per canton sinister, charged with cross Patriarch argent	Germany (H) and Czechia (H) parted per pale	Czechia (H), Slovakia (H) and azure neutral parted per counter pall	Serbia and Montenegro (H) charged with cross Croatia (H)

21 — PAGE 64-65	22 — PAGE 65	23 — PAGE 66	24 — PAGE 67
Blood brothers	*Frontiersmen*	*Kosovo*	*Wallachia*
Russia (H) and Serbia (A) quarterly	Serbia (H) charged with cross Croatia (H)	Serbia (A), Serbia and Montenegro (H) and Albania (H) tierced in pale	Romania (H) and Bulgary (H) parted and bordured per pale

25 — PAGE 68	26 — PAGE 70	27 — PAGE 71	28 — PAGE 72
Cyprus	*Istanbul 1/3*	*Istanbul 3/3*	*Kiev*
Turkey (H) and Greece (H) parted per pale	Galatasaray SK (H), Fenerbahce SK (H) and Besiktas JK (H) parted per pall	Besiktas JK (H), Galatasaray SK (H) and Fenerbahce SK (H) parted per pall	Russia (A) and Ukraine (H) parted per bend sinister

29 — PAGE 73	30 — PAGE 74	31 — PAGE 75	32 — PAGE 76
Ukraine	*St. Petersburg*	*Russo-Poland*	**Kalmar Union**
Ukraine (H) and Russia (A) parted per bend sinister	Holland (H) and Russia (A) parted per pale	Russia (A) and Poland (A) parted and bordured per pale	Denmark (H), Norway (A) and Sweden (A) tierced per dexter chevron

33 — PAGE 78	34 — PAGE 79	35 — PAGE 81	36 — PAGE 82

Finland	*Øresund*	**Blitzkrieg**	*Deutschland*
Finland (H) charged with cross Sweden (A)	Sweden (H) and Denmark (H) parted per pale	Germany (H) and Poland (H) parted per pale dancetté	Germany (A) and Germany (H) parted per pale (irreg. sinister side)

37 — PAGE 83	38 — PAGE 84	39 — PAGE 85	40 — PAGE 86

Berlin	*München*	*Ultra Udi Bremen*	*Nord derby*
Hertha BSC (H) charged with pale Germany (A)	FC Bayern München (H) and TSV 1860 München (A) quarterly	Udinese Calcio (H) Werder Bremen (H) parted per pale (irreg. rounded in chief)	Werder Bremen (A) charged with double lozenge HSV (H)

41 — PAGE 87	42 — PAGE 88	43 — PAGE 89	44 — PAGE 91

Kohlenpott	*Hamburg*	*Pirate support*	**Diets**
FC Schalke 04 (H) and Borussia Dortmund (H) barry of six	St. Pauli (H) and HSV (A) parted per fesse	Celtic FC (A) charged with canton St. Pauli supporters Tee	Germany (H) charged with Holland badge in sinister chief

45 — PAGE 92	46 — PAGE 92-93	47 — PAGE 93	48 — PAGE 94

De Opstand	*De Oorlog*	*Pour le Royaume*	*Prinsenvlag*
Spain (H) and Holland (H) parted per bend sinister	Holland (H) and Germany (H) parted per pale	France (H) and Holland (H) parted per pale	Holland (H) charged with three bars France (H & A)

Nederland	*Wilhelmina*	*Het Koningshuis*	*Fryslân*
France (3rd), Holland (A) and France (H) tierced per bend sinister	sable neutral charged with bend gules, argent, azure barry and charged with Holland badge in sinister chief	Holland (H), Germany (H) and Argentina (H) parted per counter pall bordured	Holland (A) and SC Heereveen (H) parted per chief

De Top 3	*Noord derby*	*De Klassieker*	*Mokum*
Feyenoord (H), PSV (H) and AFC Ajax (H) tierced in chevron	SC Heereveen (H) and FC Groningen (A) parted and bordured per canton	Feyenoord (A) and AFC Ajax (H) parted per pile	Israel (A) and AFC Ajax (H) parted per chevron

New Amsterdam	*Suriname*	*Bimre*	*Bijlmer*
New York Giants (H), AFC Ajax (A) and Holland (H) tierced in pale, Ajax charged with three crosses Andreas argent	England (A), Suriprofs (H) and Holland (H) tierced in pale	Holland (H) and Suriprofs (H) parted per chevron	AFC Ajax (H) charged with three crosses Andreas gold, added sleeves vert

Donkere Maroc	*Türkü*	*Blonde Maroc*	*Brabant*
Holland (H) and Morocco (H) parted per bend sinister	Holland (A) and Turkey (H) quarterly	Morocco (H) and Holland (H) bendy sinister of six	Holland (A) and checkered argent and gules neutral parted per chief

97

98

99

100

101

102

103

104

105

106

107

108

109

110

111

112

IBRAHIMOVIC

CAREERS

TAILORS
Berber Soepboer & Anne Stooker
Vladi Rapaport
Brandon Modeatelier Maja

FLOKS & BADGES
AKDR viual group
SMLX.nl

SHIRT SPONSORING
Nike Sportswear
Accent Sport Amsterdam

EDITORIAL
pages 9 — 13:
Floor Wesseling, Iranzu Baker.
pages 37 — 167:
Maarten van Heems, Bram Wits,
Melchior Bussink, Bloeme van Kessel,
Iranzu Baker, Ellen – Jane Hung.

REFERENCES
Heraldry related:
Project Gutenberg's The Handbook to
English Heraldry, by Charles Boutell.
Release Date: October 24, 2007.
www.gutenberg.org/files/23186/23186-
h/23186-h.htm
www.bloodinbloodout.nl
Football and European history related:
en.wikipedia.org
Map of Europe, pages 34 — 35:
www.lib.utexas.edu/europe1560_shepherd.jpg

ABBREVIATIONS
pages 201 — 213:
Home jerseys — (H), Away jerseys — (A)
Special Edition — (SE), Irregular — irreg.

MODELS
in order of appearance:
Jasper Blanken, Bram van Donselaar,
Ludo Nienhuis, Jaime Nayem Carrasco,
Aäron Verkruissen, Robbert Steer,
Jim Steijn, Jeffrey Croese, Rutger Odinot,
Eric Alkema, Melvin Dorn, Jeffrey Jaddoe,
Thomas van der Lee, Dherl Deekman,
Martijn van Minnen, Frank Schouten,
Willem Wesseling, Brian van Herrewaarden,
Maarten van Heems, Ronald Laurens,
Melchior Bussink, Chris Sorber,
Onno Warns, Koray Oçak, Fran Méndez,
Vladi Rapaport, Max Blank,
Michiel Schuurman, Tim van der Maas,
Constant Dullaart, Marques Malacia,
Frens Snijder, Jason Jaddoe,
Simon van Melick, Chris Baker,
Jan Huppen, Roël Zandvliet, Nordin Kraan,
Dirk van Oosterbosch, Mark Gilman,
Wouter Stelwagen, Benjamin Konjanan,
Floor Wesseling, Khoi Tran.

PHOTOGRAPHY
pages 34 — 195, 222:
Marques Malacia
pages 199 — 220:
Wouter Stelwagen

GRAPHIC DESIGN
www.floorwesseling.nl

TYPEFACES
Dolly, Gill Sans, Penumbra MM,
KoenigsbergerGotisch, Colonna MT.

CONCEPT
Floor Wesseling — Ix Opus Ada

SNEIJDER

HUNTELAAR

LINESMEN

WESSELING

SUPPORTERS

I would like to thank: Marques Malacia, Rudolf van Wezel, Ellen – Jane Hung, Aron & Soraya, Willem Wesseling, Mathieu Vrijman, Malin Lindmark Vrijman, Wouter Stelwagen, Jaime Nayem Carrasco, Chris Baker, Brian van Herrewaarden, Rutger Odinot, Emile Molin, Balázs Juhász, Mark Gilman, Michiel Schuurman, Berber Soepboer, Anne Stooker, Vladi Rapaport, Wouter van der Sluijs, Maarten van Heems, Alex Klusman, Erik van Bruggen, Lennard Booij, Simon van Melick, Melchior Bussink, Bram Wits, Bloeme van Kessel, Constant Dullaart, Wilfred Genee, Thomas Castro, Jesse Leyva, Richard Clarke, Cristiano Fagnani, Drieke Leenknegt, Andrea Zini, Juan Carlos Alfayate, Will Holder, Stuart Bailey, Jim Steijn, Jan Huppen, Koray Oçak, Roël Zandvliet, Nordin Kraan, Jasper Blanken, Bram van Donselaar, Ludo Nienhuis, Robbert Steer, Jeffrey Croese, Sara Mattens, Eric Alkema, Melvin Dorn, Jeffrey Jaddoe, Thomas van der Lee, Dherl Deekman, Aäron Verkruissen, Martijn van Minnen, Frank Schouten, Ronald Laurens, Onno Warns, Chris Sorber, Egbert Jansen, Fran Méndez, Iranzu Baker, Max Blank, Tim van der Maas, Frens Snijder, Jason Jaddoe, Dirk van Oosterbosch, Benjamin Konjanan, Khoi Tran, Guillermo Mellicovski, Mischa Booij, Onno Verbeek, Inno van Dam, Kwong Steinrath, Hamza Malouk, Tjidako Gasper, Laselle Leysner, Randy Sanchez, Roy Pieters, Bert van Dun, Niels Helleman, Melton Plummer, Tim de Wreede, Wouter de Iongh, Eric Castien, Roland Schutte, Bas Ponsioen, Wouter Staal, Pelle de Koning, Luitzen Kaspersma, Roeland Kramer, Aren van Muijen, Arthur Huizinga, Eva de Klerk, Mieke Gerritzen, Andreas Brøgger, Show Studio and Loes Wesseling van Kersen.

BIS Publishers
Building Het Sieraad
Postjesweg 1
1057 DT Amsterdam
The Netherlands

T +31 (0)20 515 02 30
F +31 (0)20 515 02 39
bis@bispublishers.nl
www.bispublishers.nl

B*IS*PUBLISHERS

ISBN 978-90-6369-244-5

Printed by Ofset Yapımevi,
Turkey.

This publication is supported by
**The Netherlands Foundation
for Visual Arts, Design and
Architecture.**